Teacher's Manual

National Textbook Company
a division of NTC/Contemporary Publishing Group
NTC Lincolnwood, Illinois USA

Contents

Chapter 5
Copyediting

Chapter 6
Design and Production

Chapter 7
Photojournalism

Chapter 8
Business and Advertising

Chapter 9
Ethics and Responsibilities

Chapter 10
Beyond the School Newspaper

The EXp3: Journalism Program

EXp3: Journalism is the first in National Textbook Company's EXp3 series. The series is designed to involve students in a field of study by focusing on three goals necessary for student success:

- **Explore your world** to understand the role of a subject in the world beyond the classroom.
- **Expand your skills** in that subject.
- **Express yourself** with those skills to make an impact on the world.

EXp3: Journalism concentrates on newspaper journalism, but the concepts and skills are applicable to all areas of journalism.

The Handbook

The *EXp3: Journalism Handbook* is one of three components in the program. As the primary student book, it will give students the nuts-and-bolts information they need to become good journalists. It's designed as a handy reference book that students can carry with them and refer to often.

At the end of each chapter are exercises organized around the EXp3 goals. For the most part, these are exercises that students can do on their own. Students are encouraged to complete the Express Yourself exercise in their Journalist's Notebook (see the student book, page xii). The Journalist's Notebook is a notebook students keep to record their learning and to get into the habit of writing down their ideas—a necessity for any successful journalist.

In addition, throughout the *Handbook* students are treated to the Press Time features, which deliver brief bites of journalism history. This integrated approach to journalism history will spark and sustain in students an interest in the development of the field of journalism.

The Workbook

The *Workbook* provides in-depth practice on journalism skills, as well as practice in critical reading and thinking. Worksheets for each chapter prompt students to apply concepts and skills used every day by journalists. Many of the worksheets include model examples from middle school, high school, and the professional press.

The Adviser Packet

The *Adviser Packet* offers you helpful articles from experienced and respected journalism advisers. It also provides you with reproducible forms and handouts for students as well as chapter quizzes. A poster and a 16-page packet on editorial cartooning are also included in the Adviser Packet.

Using This Teacher's Manual

For each chapter in the *Handbook,* this Teacher's Manual provides a variety of support and activities, beginning with Building Background. The activities in Building Background draw upon students' prior knowledge of the chapter topic and prime students with interesting background about the chapter topic.

Each major topic section of the chapters is supported with suggestions for student activities. Most can be done with no preparation or materials (other than pen/pencil and paper). And most take one average class period or less. Some, however, such as the arrangement of guest speakers, will require advance planning.

Assessment for the EXp3 exercises at the end of each chapter is also provided. Because the Express Yourself assignments are recorded in students' Journalist's Notebooks, you may wish to collect these overnight for assessment.

Many of the activities suggested in this Teacher's Manual are class or small-group discussions. This fosters a cooperative learning environment and a forum for students to learn the perspectives of other beginning journalists. Periodically, you may wish to invite other students, faculty, and staff at your school for these discussions to encourage students to consider various points of view, especially on controversial issues.

A number of the activities in the *Handbook* and in this Teacher's Manual require access to newspapers—both student papers and those from the professional press. Since some students may not have ready access at home to newspapers, keep a stack of current ones available in your classroom. You may want to subscribe to papers such as the *Chicago Tribune* and the *New York Times* as well as local papers to give students a range of samples and models.

Chapter 1

Publishing a Newspaper

Building Background

Engage students in a discussion about teamwork and leadership. First ask students to describe their experiences as part of a team. What does being part of a team require? What kinds of rules do you have to follow? What happens when some members don't do their part or when they refuse to work with others? Why does a team need a leader? Then ask students to define a successful team. Finally, have students explain how this definition might apply to working on a newspaper.

Subsequent discussion will vary, depending on whether you are starting or continuing a school paper. Encourage students to talk about why they want to be on the staff of the paper. Any previous staff members might talk about what they liked best about being on the staff and what they learned.

The Newspaper Team

Staffing the Paper: After students have studied the flow chart on page 7, ask for volunteers for jobs on the paper, emphasizing that it may be necessary to discuss specific positions with you on an individual basis. If more than one student volunteers for the post of editor-in-chief, for example, you'll want to evaluate each student's qualifications. (A worksheet on staff positions is included in the *Workbook* and a staff application form is included in the *Adviser Packet.)*

If the school doesn't provide cameras, photographers will need to use their own; however, the newspaper budget should supply film.

If additional staff members need to be recruited, students can work together to design a help-wanted flyer for posting in school.

Naming Papers: If no paper has previously been published, or if students want to change the name of the paper, have them brainstorm possible names. Tell them that names of newspapers traditionally focus on the frequency of publication *(Daily News),* thoroughness of coverage *(Chronicle, Review, Ledger, Globe),* brilliance of reporting *(Inquirer, Star, Sun, Beacon),* or commitment to certain values *(The Cleveland Plain-Dealer, The Detroit Free Press).* Others emphasize a geographic area *(The Nashville Tennessean, The Portland Oregonian).* Still others simply use traditional newspaper names *(Gazette, Journal, Post, Times, Tribune).* Many student newspapers have informal names, often named after the school mascot.

The Readers

Student Reading Habits: As a class, have students chart their newspaper reading habits. How often do they read a paper? What types of papers do they read? Why those papers? What types of stories do they read and why? What types of stories do they avoid reading and why? Ask someone to record the comments in two columns on the chalkboard: types of stories most students read and types of stories most students don't read. Establish that their comments may indicate what students would like to read.

The Editorial Board: Ask students to decide who should be on the editorial board and then to establish a regular time and place for the board to meet. If they think board members will need to be reminded about meetings, students should decide how this can be accomplished.

The Process

Deadlines: Ask all students, whether members of the editorial board or not, to work on a deadline schedule for the paper. The staff may be divided into small groups, with experienced and inexperienced staff members working together.

Visit to the Printers: If the paper is printed commercially, arrange for students to visit the press and talk to the printer. If possible, arrange the visit during a time when students can see the press in action.

Assessment

Explore Your World Ask various students to name the sections in the newspapers they read. What assumptions did they make about the interest of the readers from the sections of the paper? from the advertising? Make sure students support their assumptions with concrete examples. Ask each student to name one story they read in a paper and explain how that story reflects the paper's readership.

Depending on whether students have read a weekly newspaper, a small-town daily, a metropolitan daily, or a national paper, such as *USA Today,* their answers to the discussion questions will vary.

Expand Your Skills Ask students to submit the lists they made; note the skills they say they have and need.

Express Yourself If there has been no previous school paper, adjust this assignment and have students write a letter to prospective readers asking for opinions on what they would like to see in a paper. Assess grammar, usage, and mechanics as well as how students express themselves.

Chapter 2

News Gathering

Building Background

Tell students that there are about 1500 professional newspapers in the United States but they don't always feature the same stories on any one day or give the same amount of space to a particular story. Ask students why this might be.

Establish that editorial boards regularly decide which stories readers will most want or need to know about. The staff of a school paper must make similar evaluations. Ask students which of the following topics they would cover in a story for a school paper with a final deadline the third Friday of the month, and why:

- the U. S. President's trip abroad
- the First Lady's visit to the school on the Monday before the deadline
- a new policy regarding school uniforms
- national reading test scores
- a new basketball coach at the school
- a former student who is now a singer with a top band
- a bank robbery in the town the day before the deadline

Defining News

Classifying Newsworthy Stories: Ask students in small groups to brainstorm for 10 or 15 minutes about possible stories for their paper, judging the newsworthiness of stories by applying the elements of news on page 17 of the *Handbook.* Suggest that they may want to recall the various sections and stories they read earlier in professional papers. One student from each group should list the possible stories on the board. Then have the class designate which stories they would label hard news and which soft news. Make sure students explain why they categorize the stories as they do.

Finding Stories and Sources

Guest Reporters: Invite one or more reporters from a local newspaper to talk to the class about their jobs. If possible, invite a sports reporter, a news reporter, and a reporter or reviewer of entertainment events. (On a small paper, one reporter may fill all of these roles.) Ask students to jot down questions ahead of time to ask the reporters. Possible questions might include these: What is the most interesting story you have recently covered? How did you learn about the story? What sources did you consult? How do you evaluate your sources? Have you ever written a story that was not published? How did you learn to be a journalist?

Interviewing

Role playing: All students will benefit by role playing before they actually interview a source. Have students in pairs take turns interviewing each other. This activity may take two class periods. The source may be asked about his or her background, interests, and achievements. Be sure to allow students time to research their sources first. Students should follow the steps on pages 26–33. Follow up by asking students to evaluate how they performed (their strengths and weaknesses) before, during, and after the interviews.

Assessment

Explore Your World Ask students to jot down the questions they think the reporter might have asked to get the information in the story they were asked to read. Evaluate how perceptive the questions are and whether students have grasped the types of questions needed to fully report a story.

Expand Your Skills Ask each student to speak briefly about the person they interviewed to determine whether they have focused on a newsworthy story.

Express Yourself Determine whether students, especially shy ones, need more encouragement or practice in interviewing before they conduct an interview for the news paper. If initial enthusiasm on the part of some students has waned, assure them that the *Handbook* will help them to become successful members of the newspaper staff.

Chapter 3

Journalistic Writing

Building Background

Tell students that journalistic writing is somewhat different from the writing they have usually done in school:

- Good journalistic writing is not fiction, but it's colorful.
- It's not poetry, but it's rhythmical.
- It's not an essay, but it's well organized.
- It's not a journal entry, but sometimes can express opinions.
- Good journalistic writing appeals to many types of readers, not just to teachers or other class members.

Mention that excellence in professional journalistic writing in the United States is rewarded by annual awards called Pulitzer Prizes. Some winners receive gold medals. Others, in various categories, receive checks for $3000 each. Refer students to the Press Time feature about Joseph Pulitzer on page 37 of the *Handbook*.

Qualities of Journalistic Writing

Checking Accuracy: Read the sentences listed below aloud. Ask for volunteers to tell which information they should double-check in each sentence and what resources they could use to check the information. (Underlining indicates spellings of proper nouns, dates, and times that students should check.) You may want to have students copy the sentences as you dictate them.

- <u>Anne</u> Brown was born in <u>Dubuque</u> in <u>1956.</u>
- She attended Willow School from <u>1967 to 1969.</u>
- She moved with her parents to <u>Cincinnati,</u> where she attended college.
- Her first big acting job was in the play *Plaza <u>Suite.</u>*
- She will appear at The Book <u>Shop October 20</u> at <u>1 p.m.</u> to sign copies of her autobiography.

Facts and Opinions: Ask one or two students to give an example of an opinion statement. Ask two other students to give an example of a factual statement.

Discuss how language used to express an opinion differs from language used to express a fact and have students cite specific words or phrases from the examples provided that make one a statement of opinion as opposed to a statement of fact.

If you'd like to extend this activity, bring in several news stories from local papers. Have students work in small groups to identify opinion words or phrases that should not appear in a news story. They can draw a line through these. Then have them read their story for the rest of the class, with and without the opinion words and phrases. If there isn't class time for this activity, students can find their own news stories and do this as a homework assignment. If time allows, they can present their stories to the rest of the class.

Rewriting for Better Writing: Ask student to write down the following sentences. Then ask them to rewrite each sentence to avoid clichés, boring verb constructions, passive voice, and wordiness:

- There is a sparkling new trophy in the display case in the east hallway.
- The trophy was won by the soccer team.
- The trophy was presented Friday evening at 7 p.m. in the gym to soccer captain James Hughes. He was applauded by parents and students.
- Coach Carl Baird congratulated team members and, last but not least, thanked all parents.
- Every game was won by the team this year, an unbroken record, but there are three graduating students, all seniors.

Writing Leads

Lead Practice: Divide the class into four small groups and give each group the facts listed below. Using the facts, ask one group to write a summary lead, one to write a storytelling lead, one to write a blind lead, and one to write a punch lead. Tell them that they don't need to use all the facts in a lead. Much of the information would appear later in the story. Ask students to save their leads.

- Four new students in the seventh grade are from Mexico.
- Their names are Ana Hernandez, Carlos Castillo, Maria Ramos, and Juan Cardenas.
- All of them attended school in Mexico before arriving in the United States last spring.
- Ana and Carlos speak some English. Maria and Juan are still learning to speak English.
- All of these students came with their families from the state of Sonora.
- Carlos had visited an uncle in the United States a year ago.
- Ana and Maria did not know each other before, but they're fast becoming friends.
- Juan says he is eager to learn all he can about the States.
- Both Carlos and Juan like to watch sports on television.
- Ana likes to read when she has free time. Maria is learning to cook. She also takes care of a younger brother and sister.
- Carlos and Ana like fast food. Maria and Juan are not so sure they do.
- Some students at Willow School have taken Spanish. They'll know how to say *Buenos dias.*

Handling Quotes

Taking Notes on Quotes: Remind students about the value of using a shorthand system to take notes during an interview. Relying entirely on tape recorders is risky, and trying to write complete words can cause them to miss information. When they need to record a speaker's exact words, they should always start and end the remarks with quotation marks so that they can refer later to where the quotes begin and end.

Ask students to practice taking notes on quotes while watching a television news program. They should take notes on who the person is (if identified) and what that person says, using their own system of shorthand. For an in-class activity, videotape portions of a news program and play them for the class so that everyone can takes note on the same program. Then have students compare their quotes.

Organizing the Story

Story of a Typical Day: Prepare students to take notes for a story on a typical day in the life of a student in their school. Then ask a class member to briefly describe what he or she does on a typical weekday from the time the alarm goes off until bedtime (taking no more than 10 minutes). Tell students to jot down any questions they have and to ask them at the end of the speaker's presentation.

Afterwards, ask the class to tell in what basic order the speaker told about the day. Did the speaker vary the order in any way? What seemed to be the most important or interesting part of the day? the least important? What questions would students like to ask to flesh out the story? What are the 5 W's and the H in this story? Finally, ask students to tell how they might organize the story: chronologically? starting with the most important part of the day first? starting with a quotation?

Writing Headlines

Misleading Headlines: Headlines have probably caused readers more confusion and amusement than any other part of a paper, often because headline writers have to compress the main point of a story into as few words as possible. The following are illustrations of some types of pitfalls that await headline writers. Ask students to tell what is wrong with each headline and how it might be corrected.

Principal finds class alone

Class trips up

Player leaves bench leaning on manager

Used-book drives off

Math teacher never added

Cafeteria staff grows larger

Student sees mouse studying in library

Shrinking students cause cancellation of French

Headline for the Lead Story: Ask students to refer to the lead they wrote and saved on the four new students from Mexico. Have them now write a headline for the story. Post the headlines.

Writing Cutlines

Analyzing Cutlines: Have each student bring to class at least five photographs with cutlines (not the accompanying stories) from several sections of daily or weekly newspapers. Divide the class into small groups to examine the photos and cutlines, noting how many of the photos gathered were of people.

Help guide discussion by asking the following questions as you move about the room: Were the people identified? Did the cutline help to explain why the people were newsworthy? Were most of the photos of groups or of individual people? What kinds of people dominated the news? Were any cutlines confusing? How many photos showed some kind of action? Did the cutlines explain what was happening? How many of the photos were of something besides people? Did the cutlines help to explain what made these photos newsworthy? Do any of the cutlines state the obvious? What are some examples of strong, active verbs used in the cutlines?

Assessment

Explore Your World Discuss with students the conclusions they reached after skimming the daily newspaper. Look for evidence that they have understood summary and creative leads, different types of quotes, editorializing, and the functions of cutlines.

Expand Your Skills Ask students to hand in their rewrites of leads and headlines for this assignment, and evaluate grammar, usage, and mechanics. Pay special attention to how the headlines abide by the rules on page 81.

Express Yourself Assess the objectivity and organization of the story and whether students punctuated quotes correctly and included attribution as necessary.

Chapter 4

Types of Journalistic Writing

Building Background

Tell students that Chapter 4 in the *Handbook* covers four main types of journalistic writing—news, features, sports, and editorials. Explain that these terms will be defined in the chapter. Then ask students to explain what they think each type is like.

Finally, have students classify the following stories into types, using whatever terms they like at this point:

- a story about when and where auditions are to be held for a school play
- an interview with the director of the school play
- a story about the local historical society
- the results of a survey about cafeteria lunch preferences
- a story about overcrowded classrooms
- a story about how cheerleaders are chosen

News

Planning News Coverage: To help students plan various types of news stories, ask them to think about the following two events and to discuss the questions:

Event #1: *A December 3 concert by King School Orchestra is scheduled for 7:30 p.m. in the auditorium.*

- How might you handle an advance story about the event? as a news brief? in a boxed school calendar? as part of a roving reporter?
- Who might be responsible for an advance story? a general-assignment reporter? a beat reporter?
- What can be included in an advance story that is more than an announcement of the event?
- Can a student-achievement story be tied in with news of the concert?

Event #2: *Vandalism in the girls' locker room results in theft of clothes, graffiti on walls, and water damage. The event occurs two weeks before the paper is put to bed.*

- How might you handle a coverage story about this event?
- Who might be assigned to the story? the sports section editor? a beat reporter? A sports reporter?
- Should a photo or photos accompany the story?
- What kind of information might be included in a sidebar?
- Is this an opportunity for in-depth reporting? If so, is there time?
- What questions should reporters ask and of whom?

Ask someone to record on the board questions students would want to ask about the vandalism story and the people who might have the answers. Students should suggest some of the following questions: Has anyone been charged with the vandalism? (police) Did the vandals break in? (police) Has this ever happened before? (principal, police) Has it happened in other schools? (police) What kind of investigation took place? (principal, police, coach) Has the damage been repaired or cleaned up? (custodian, principal, coach) What is the cost of the damage, and how will it be paid for? (principal, school board president)

Features

Featurizing News: Ask students to think back to the assignments they did for the "News" section. Ask these questions: What feature stories might accompany the news story on the orchestra concert? What feature stories could grow out of the story about school vandalism?

Analyzing Features: Distribute copies of a feature story from a daily newspaper and ask students to analyze it. You might choose a story providing historical background on a current news event, a feature on a newsworthy person, a feature on some aspect of entertainment or the media, or a feature on the environment. Exclude reviews since they're editorials.

Student discussion should center around the following questions:

- How does the headline indicate that the story is soft news?
- Why did the editors or the writer assume that the story has human interest? Do you agree?
- Does the story have a news peg? What is it?
- Is the lead a good one? Why or why not?
- Does the story create a particular mood? If so, what?
- Does the writer include anecdotes or dialogue? If so, is it effective?
- What type of feature is this? (See page 90.)
- How effective is the ending?

Sports

Sports Sources: Ask students to list types of people, other than players and coaches, that are associated with team sports, and who might make interesting sources for sports features. (Umpires, referees, cheerleaders, band members, grounds keepers, equipment managers, and fans are all potential sources for features.)

Sports Coverage: Have students brainstorm nonteam or noncompetitive sports and recreation they could cover as well as students they know who are involved in these sports. (Students who enjoy hiking, camping, cycling, horseback riding, skateboarding, skating, jogging, sailing, swimming, and canoeing are all good sources.) Staff members might also discuss whether they would consider expanding sports coverage to include board, computer, and video games.

Winners and Losers: Author John R. Tunis wrote that "Americans believe in the happy ending. It's hard to make them accept the fact that if two football teams meet, one of them is pretty sure to lose." Ask students to discuss the difficulties of writing objectively about winners and losers. Challenge them to suggest strategies that will help sports writers remain objective about the athletes from their school and those from opposing schools.

Reading Sports Literature: Students may enjoy reading *Sports in Literature* by Bruce Emra (copyright 1991, 2000), published by NTC/Contemporary Publishing Group, Inc. Many types of sports features, as well as fiction and poetry about sports, are included.

Editorials

Editorial-Page Analysis: Ask students to bring to class at least three editorial and op-ed pages from a particular professional newspaper. In small groups, have them determine whether the purpose of the editorials is to persuade, praise, explain, or entertain. Ask each group to locate and summarize editorial policy information on the pages, including policies about letters to the editor. Next, ask them to determine how many columnists are represented, as well as which columns are the most well written and why. Finally, ask them to study an editorial cartoon present on the pages and summarize its point.

The Politics of Caricatures: Although well-known people are presumably accustomed to being caricatured, school newspaper readers may not be amused at caricatures of themselves, especially if a cartoon accompanies a critical editorial. Tell students to assess the possible consequences of publishing a caricature of a school newspaper reader in their newspaper.

School Subjects: Assign one or more interested students to practice writing editorials about or depicting in editorial cartoons such subjects as overcrowded, overheated, or underheated classrooms; interiors of overstuffed lockers; unruly fan behavior at a sports or entertainment event; excessive noise inside or outside the school; or students' attitudes about homework. Then have them analyze each other's work, taking care to be constructive in their criticism. Some students might like to try drawing a cartoon strip based on school situations.

Cartoonists On Line: In addition to studying editorial and comics pages, interested students will enjoy accessing the web sites of cartoonists to study styles of drawing and situations depicted. Encourage them to share printouts of their favorites on a bulletin board.

Assessment

Explore Your World This assignment can be evaluated informally. Encourage students to talk about what they have read, referring to the questions asked. Make sure students cite specific examples from the stories they read to support their answers.

Expand Your Skills Ask for comments about student experiences with this assignment. Did they have trouble deciding which type of story to write? When they started to write, did they feel they had enough information? What problems, if any, did they encounter? Talk through these questions in class.

Express Yourself Most students will not have trouble with this assignment. Ask them to turn in their columns for your evaluation. Look particularly for logical progression of ideas and adherence to the subject. Return the columns to students with suggestions for improvement. You may wish to submit them to the editorial board for consideration about publishing some of them. Assure students that if their columns are not published, they'll have time to revise them or to write new columns for submission.

Chapter 5

Copyediting and Proofreading

Building Background

Tell students that all copy needs to be edited, simply because everyone makes mistakes. Use this example to illustrate the relative ease of correcting mistakes with modern technology: Monks, who copied religious manuscripts slowly and painstakingly by hand before the invention of type, made errors that are in museums for all to see. Today one can detect letters on these pages that were scraped off and corrected, as well as errors that were never corrected, such as repeated words and incomplete sentences. Ask students why they think the monks didn't correct all the mistakes. They may suggest that the message was considered more important than accuracy or that the prospect of recopying whole pages with a sharpened quill pen would have been a daunting task. Or they may know that vellum (animal skin prepared to use as paper) was very expensive.

Then prompt students to compare the difficulty of making corrections in the past to making corrections today. Discuss the difficulty of making corrections using early printing methods.

Make sure that every staff member has a copy of the stylebook for the paper. Or have them refer to the Stylebook that begins on page 245 of the *Handbook.*

Copyediting

Backing Up: Remind students that when they turn over a story to a copy editor to be edited electronically, they need to keep a hard copy or a copy on disk of the original story in case the editor's copy disappears, either through carelessness or a power failure. Have each student prepare a paper or electronic file in which to store back-ups of all their stories.

Copyediting Practice: Provide students with the sentences below and ask them which facts they would check. Then ask them to correct each sentence if it contains errors or goes against your paper's stylebook. Ask them to write after each sentence what resources or tools they used to make corrections. They should use standard copyediting symbols, such as those on pages 144–145 in the *Handbook.* Note: One item has no errors.

- Ramona Berkeley, 8th grader, was the winner of the state essay contest sponsored by the American Legion. Ramona is not the first Berkley winner of the contest. Her sister Pam won last year.
- Five members of the tenth-grade class recieved complementary tickets to the Husky game.

- Girls' basketball coach Ellen Baker said that anything found laying on the floor or benches in the locker room will be thrown out.
- Joe Shoemaker, 6th grader, still has the stray dog he found in the parking lot October 14. Call Joe at 555-5521 if you know the owner.
- Junior Jessica Wong will compete in the state gymnastic finals in the Spring.
- Among the new books in the library is "The Life and Death of Crazy Horse" by Russell Freedman. The book tells about the Sioux leader who fought bravely at the Battle of Little Big Horn.
- The seventh grade class raised forty dollars at their car wash October 3.
- Principle Nancy Estevez is out of the hospital. She says that she hopes to be back at school before to long.
- The Eschbach twins, Myra and Marilyn, both freshman, will be moving to PA at semester break.
- Board member Lisa Kaplan voted for an increase in spending for music education, Sydney Monroe voted against the measure.

Proofreading

Proofing Tips: Provide students with the following proofreading tips that professional proofreaders use. Point out that these tips will come in handy to proofread any of their writing, for the school newspaper and beyond.

- Read the story or article out loud, slowly. Carefully pronounce everything you see.
- Place a ruler under each line as you read.
- Read the story or article against the original copy. Compare the final draft sentence by sentence against the draft from which it was copied.
- Read the essay backward from the end to the beginning. Examine each sentence separately. (This helps keep the content from distracting the proofreader.)

Proofreading Practice: In addition to the proofreading activity in the Workbook, provide students with some real world proofreading activities. Bring in several copies of the local newspaper(s), or have students bring in their own, and have them proofread one of the articles using one or more of the proofreading techniques provided here. They can use the appropriate copyediting symbols on pages 126–127 to mark any errors they find in the copy.

If your time allows, take a story from the local paper and recopy it with errors. Make copies for students to proofread, marking any errors with the appropriate symbol. To check their work, pass out the original version of the story.

Assessment

Explore Your World Ask students to focus particularly on whether stories seem well written or confusing. Forced to copy fit, editors sometimes trim too much from within a story or from the end of a story, making it difficult to follow. Readers may also notice typographical errors or a story that supposedly jumps to an inside page but is missing entirely or found on a page other than the one cited. Make an informal evaluation of whether students truly examined the stories they read.

Expand Your Skills Check students' work to determine their level of achievement. Even ambitious students may not have the background at this time to produce a well-written story correctly edited and proofread. If you conclude that the work of some students will always have to be rewritten or heavily edited, you can direct them to other positions where they can be successful staff members until their writing skills improve—possibly through a better mastery of English or practice at writing news briefs or sidebars.

Express Yourself Evaluate student entries by determining how much they have understood the copy editor's job. Some students might like to assume the imaginary role of a copy editor reading manuscript that monks have copied in their illuminated manuscripts (as mentioned in the introductory paragraph of this chapter in the Teacher's Manual).

Chapter 6

Design and Production

Building Background

Mention that most newspaper readers, unless they're journalists or graphic artists, pay little attention to a newspaper's design. If they have difficulty reading a story or find a page layout confusing, however, they'll simply stop reading that paper. Students will be learning how to be experts about what makes a newspaper easy to read, graphically interesting, and, thus, eagerly awaited by its readers.

Tell students that most early newspapers were owned and published by printers, who had familiarity with type, ink, and presses, but little idea about appealing layout. Until the early 1980s, most newspapers consisted of rows of gray columns topped by bold headlines. Big stories were accented by a sketch or black and white photo, but even photos weren't able to be reproduced in newspapers until the late 1800s. Direct them to the feature about *USA Today* on page 153 and its impact on newspaper design.

Design Basics

Assessing Principles of Design: Before bringing to class the major sections of two daily papers, cut off the names of the papers and mark out the page numbers. Then insert some the sections of one newspaper within the other so that there are still two papers. Ask students to tell whether each paper has unity. Students should be able to see that the pages seem unrelated because they're. Reveal what you have done, and ask one or two students to reassemble the papers more or less properly, which should be easy to do if students have noted the design similarities among pages.

Next, ask students to point to the dominant element on the first three pages of the first section of each newspaper. Then ask them to find examples of contrast and repetition. Ask whether they feel most pages are balanced. Finally, ask for a show of hands to tell which paper seems better designed.

Layout

Layout Practice: This activity may take two class periods since most students will have to refer to information in the *Handbook* from time to time.

Provide students with the following bulleted items, and have them do thumbnails (page 165 of the *Handbook)* of a front page or an interior news page for their paper, selecting from the items listed below. Then distribute several grid sheets to each student. (If there are no grid sheets for your paper, prepare some for them, using as a guide the format of the school paper.) Have students use the grid sheets to prepare dummies based on their thumbnails. Suggest that they follow the tips on page 164. Tell them that they don't have to follow their thumbnails exactly (they're only rough sketches) and can change their minds about layouts.

As they prepare their thumbnails and dummies, remind them to consider which news is front-page news and which could be moved to an interior page or a section page. They should also make judgements about size of headlines, based on the importance of the story.

Column inches cited for each story refer to what has been written. The length can be decreased by no more than three inches and can't be increased.

- A story on completion of the new gym—approximately 9 inches. Byline needed. Horizontal photo of construction available. Cutline needed if used.
- Club events schedule for next month—approximately 2 inches.
- An interview with new student teacher—approximately 10 inches. Byline needed. Mug shot available. Cutline needed if used.
- A story on upcoming free flu shots—approximately 2 inches. Cartoon available.
- A story on books recently acquired by library—approximately 7 inches. Byline needed.
- A story on upcoming band concert—approximately 5 inches. Horizontal photo of entire band available. Cutline needed if used.

- A story on environmental club visit to zoo—approximately 3 inches. Byline needed. Illustration available.
- A story on architectural firm that designed the gym—approximately 8 inches.
- News briefs—approximately 3 inches.
- Roving reporter—approximately 3 inches.

Post layouts so students can compare them and explain reasons for their decisions. Have students save their layouts.

Typography

Specifying Type: Tell students that if their paper is printed by a commercial printer, they must be sure that the printer has the fonts and sizes that students want.

Ask students to specify body type and display type (for headlines, bylines, and cutlines) on the layouts they created in the "Layout" section (page 19 in this *Teacher's Manual).* They can choose type from sample books available from a printer or from electronic typeface directories (many of which are available on line). Make sure they specify the font (not just the typeface) as well as the alignment. They should also specify the leading for the body type. As they make their choices, refer them to the tips on Top-Notch Typography on page 178 of the *Handbook.*

Graphics

Choosing Graphics with a Purpose: Ask students to suggest what kinds of graphics they could use to illustrate the following stories. Make sure students determine what purpose(s) each graphic will serve (to emphasize, to distinguish, to communicate, to clarify, to unify, to identify).

- A feature to help incoming students get acquainted with the school.
- A news story about state funding for the arts *versus* funding for sports for the past three years.
- A news story about participants in the science fair.
- A feature about the formation of a drama club.
- A feature about available summer jobs.
- A feature about nutrition guidelines for teenage weight-lifters.
- A feature about student film making.
- A news story about a student art exhibit.
- A feature about foreign exchange students.
- An interview with a former school athlete now playing professional sports.

Ad Layout

Designing an Ad: Have students write and design a four-inch display ad, using measurements taken from the grid for their paper. They may advertise any product or service. They should use a graphic and spec the type fonts and sizes. Each ad must include the elements described on page 188 of the Handbook, and should follow the tips on page 189.

Students may simply dummy the ad. If they have access to a computer, they may prepare a finished ad. Remind them that the purpose of the ad must be clear, the layout should be visually attractive, and the reader should be told how or where to obtain the product or service. Post finished ads on the bulletin board and critique them, stressing constructive criticism.

Some students might like to make copies of the ads and try laying out one or two pages showing ads, news, and feature copy. Make sure they follow the guidelines for placing ads on page 190 of the *Handbook.*

Paste-up

Paste-up in Process: If possible, schedule a time for the newspaper staff to visit the offices of a professional paper to see the paste-up and printing process. Students may be interested in seeing the many steps involved as pages are prepared for plate making during "pre-press."

Assessment

Explore Your World Assess students' understanding of basic design principles, the goals of newspaper design, and effective ads by having them explain why their examples demonstrate good design. Invite students to compare the layouts they chose.

Expand Your Skills Engage the class in a discussion of the students' suggestions to change or incorporate different typography and graphics into their own paper. If the class reaches a consensus on any changes, have volunteers prepare sample pages to test the changes. If the changes are successful in sample pages, have the design editor incorporate these systematically into the paper's design and production guide (if you have one) and try them out in the next issue.

Express Yourself Evaluate this assignment both on design and on content. Invite students to do peer assessment to see if others feel their ads represent themselves clearly and effectively.

Chapter 7

Photojournalism

Building Background

Mention that some of the most famous news photographs of the 20th century appeared not in newspapers but in *Life* magazine, founded in 1936, which for many years was a weekly publication. If possible, provide students with several issues of *Life* magazine to look at. Encourage interested students to study the work of some of the following *Life* photographers: Margaret Bourke-White, Robert Capa, Yousuf Karsh, and Eli Reed.

Also, tell students that each year *The World Almanac* publishes news photos of notable events from the previous year. If you have access to current editions, make them available to students.

Note: Whole-class activities may not always be possible as students study this chapter in the *Handbook* because of unavailability of cameras or individual student's abilities.

Photo Coverage

Photo Functions: To get students thinking about the functions of photos, pose the following questions and have students brainstorm possible answers: How might you communicate test anxiety in a photo? Which types of news stories might seem more credible if accompanied by a photo? How could you capture the vitality of familiar school settings with photography? For example, how could you use photographs to accompany stories about the cafeteria, the science lab, the gym, or the library?

Planning a Shoot: Have students role play a meeting between a section editor, reporter, and photographer planning a photo shoot. The story under discussion is about the various ways students get to school. Students should discuss the angle and how the story might be enhanced with photographs. If you have a photo assignment form, have them fill it out. If you don't, either have each group create one, following the guidelines on page 201 of the *Handbook,* or use the one included in the *Adviser Packet.*

Camera Operation

Getting Familiar with Cameras: If students have little familiarity with cameras, bring at least one camera (several would be preferable) to class. Show and explain the various parts. Then allow each student to take a picture of a person or an object or scene in and/or out of the classroom. Tell students that they'll have more opportunities to improve their technique as they study this chapter. If students are sharing a camera for this exercise, ask them to keep a record of the number of the picture, the subject, and the exposure settings (as described on page 214 of the *Handbook).* This will help everyone remember which student took which picture.

Students who are already fairly sophisticated photographers can compare their cameras and any photos they've taken.

Photo Scrapbook: Ask all students to be on the alert for published photos in magazines and newspapers that they consider particularly effective. If they own the publications, they can clip the photos and start a scrapbook.

Photo Analysis: Have each student photograph the same indoor or outdoor scenes from different viewpoints and using different exposures and depths of field. Photos can then be analyzed for technical qualities and their ability to communicate news. This exercise can be repeated throughout study of this chapter.

Lighting

Photo Exhibits: Libraries and galleries frequently have photo exhibits. If there are any in your area, arrange for a class trip to visit them. They may spark students' enthusiasm for exhibiting their own work in the school or community.

Lighting Experiments: Ask photographers to experiment with lighting by photographing the same subject using various lighting directions and under various lighting conditions. After processing, have students compare and critique the photos.

Composition

Special Subjects: Tell students that since so much news revolves around people involved in events, most photojournalists specialize in shooting these types of scenes. Some photographers, however, specialize in certain types of images, such as architecture, still life arrangements of objects, animals, nature, urban life, portraits, and sports.

Urge students to experiment with composition using a subject they feel comfortable with—perhaps the family dog, the house or apartment building they live in, a friend, or a dish on a kitchen table. Remind them to follow the guidelines for composition outlined on pages 221–223 in the *Handbook*. Post their best efforts on the classroom bulletin board.

Processing and Editing

Cropping and Sizing: If staffers have assembled a number of developed photos, spread them out on a table and have them experiment with marking them for a printer to crop and size. If students can crop and size on a computer, monitor their efforts. Then have the staff analyze the effectiveness of their work.

Guest Photographer: Invite a photojournalist to talk to the class about his or her work. Students might ask the person to bring examples of recent shots and tell something about the circumstances surrounding the shots, how many photos the person took, and why a particular photo was or was not chosen for publication. Students will also be interested in the photojournalist's career path.

Assessment

Explore Your World Evaluate students' comments informally to gauge their ability to make judgments about newsworthiness, functions, lighting, focus, and composition.

Expand Your Skills Examine student photos to determine what they've learned and what they still need to learn. If some students aren't comfortable with how to operate a camera, spend some extra time with them, or have a more competent student do so.

Express Yourself Students' descriptions will provide good clues to their creativity and awareness of the types of assignments possible.

You may want to suggest that students look through magazines and newspapers if they're having difficulty coming up with ideas.

Chapter 8

Business and Advertising

Building Background

Some students may have had experience as a class or club treasurer. If so, ask them to tell what their duties were.

Discuss with students the typical sources of income for their paper and tell them whether the previous year's paper, if any, had a balanced budget.

Remind students what they learned in Chapter 1 about the relationship of readers to the advertising that supports many papers (page 10 in the *Handbook).*

Although the school paper may be partly financed through ads and subscriptions, tell students that they must still demonstrate good business sense in order to encourage funding from other resources.

Budgeting

Keeping a Daily Ledger: Have students in small groups practice keeping a daily ledger and a simplified running account; that is, an account in which they record information from a daily ledger. Give them the hypothetical information listed below to enter into the daily ledger. Ask them to record the information in income or expense columns, and then ask them to compute the daily balance in a balance column. Their running account should include columns for accounts receivable and accounts payable.

Have them total income, expenses, and amount receivable at the end of the month: Total income should be $320.00, total expenses should be $423.56, and amount receivable should be $200.00 at the end of October.

- Oct. 1; balance from September $192.95
- Oct. 2; photocopying Sept. issue; $40.00
- Oct. 3; laser printer paper; $12.05
- Oct. 4; phone bill; $14.35
- Oct. 5; misc. office supplies; $20.00
- Oct. 6; B.J.'s Pizza ad (prepaid); $40.00
- Oct. 9; Baker's Shoes ad; $80.00
- Oct. 10; film; $15.75
- Oct. 11; subscription/daily paper; $150.00
- Oct. 12; camera repair; $50.00
- Oct. 13; Ed's Sporting Goods ad (prepaid); $80.00
- Oct. 16; print cartridges; $75.16
- Oct. 17; Harry's Bike Shop ad; $40.00
- Oct. 18; Amy's Book Store ad; $40.00
- Oct. 19; LuAn's School of Dance ad (prepaid); $40.00
- Oct. 20; doughnuts; $5.75
- Oct. 23; film; $7.50

- Oct. 24; Al's Electronics ad (prepaid); $80.00
- Oct. 25; Duke's Deli ad; $40.00
- Oct. 26; postage; $30.00
- Oct. 30; bus fare; $3.00
- Oct. 31; Gina's Ice Cream ad (prepaid); $80.00

Advertising

Student Market Survey: Students might like to conduct a market survey on student spending—what students buy, where they buy it, and how much they spend monthly. The survey might include questions about the influence of advertising on student spending. Have interested students prepare an infographic of the results.

Role Playing Ad Sales: Have students prepare an ad contract (per page 240 of the *Handbook),* and pair off to role play the ad-sales process—from contacting the owner of a business through the sales presentation and filling out of the contract. The salesperson should be prepared to answer questions about the ad rates, publication dates, and student spending habits.

Distribution

Increasing Circulation: Ask pairs of students to create a display ad or a poster to help increase circulation (readership) of their school paper. The benefits of reading the school paper should be clear in the ad or poster. Include the best ads in the next issue of your paper or the local newspaper and hang the best posters in prominent places in your school and community.

Assessment

Explore Your World Evaluate this assignment informally through class discussion, or ask students to submit their lists of the range of products and services they found in ads and their conclusions about the readers and ad placement. Students might also be asked to contrast ads in local papers with ads in metropolitan dailies. Students in rural areas, for example, will find distinct differences between services advertised in a local newspaper and services advertised in a metropolitan paper.

Expand Your Skills If students call on a potential client, they can be evaluated on whether they in fact succeeded in obtaining an ad. If they did not, ask them for any reasons the prospective advertiser gave for not buying an ad, and have the rest of the class brainstorm possible further approaches to the client. If they role-play, evaluate their sales technique. Were they confident? knowledgeable? polite?

Express Yourself Students who have delivered papers will have particular insights into this assignment. Cartoonists might like to accompany their writing with a cartoon strip. Evaluate the assignment for creativity and understanding of the circulation process.

Chapter 9

Ethics and Responsibilities

Building Background

Students may know about press censorship in many parts of the world and about the risks that journalists take to report the news. Tell them that President Franklin Roosevelt created the Office of Censorship in 1941 at the start of World War II. Roosevelt wrote that "all Americans abhor censorship, just as they abhor war, but the experience of this and of all other nations has demonstrated that some degree of censorship is essential in war time, and we are at war."

Communication to and from the United States by mail, cable, and radio was examined and sometimes not allowed to go through. Later, editors and publishers were warned against printing inappropriate news about troop movements, planes, weather, and so on. The Office of Censorship ended after Japan surrendered in 1945.

Prior to that, after World War I, the Sedition Act of 1918 made it illegal to mail materials critical of the government. This temporary act halted the mailing of the New York Times and other newspapers.

Ask students how the military and government today might unofficially censor news during a war. Is such censorship justifiable?

Freedom of the Press

The Impact of Hazelwood: Assign students to research the circumstances surrounding the *Hazelwood School District* v. *Kuhlmeier* case. Then lead a debate with students in which they take sides on the issues involved in student press freedom. Ask them to speculate on what types of material might be considered "reasonably" related to education concerns, and so become subject to censorship under *Hazelwood.*

Making Decisions: Students may encounter situations involving freedom of the press that will require them to make careful decisions. Situations of these types should be discussed before they occur. Initiate discussion on the following hypothetical situations, referring students to the *Handbook* for information on unprotected speech and defenses against libel, as appropriate:

- During an interview, which you have on tape, your source makes a racist remark in the middle of an important, relevant quote. Should you include this remark in your story? What can you do?
- You're editing a review of a school play that leads with this sentence: "The only thing

worse than the acting in the school production of *Oklahoma!* was the set design." What will you do and why?

- A teacher in your school has been arrested for drunken driving. Will you print the story? Where will you get your information?
- A student in your school is alleged to have stolen computer equipment and is in police custody. Will you print the story?
- Your paper prints a news story stating that three students, who are named, have been suspended from school. Your source is a teacher, who told you the students were suspended, but the teacher was mistaken. What will you do?
- You've misidentified a student in a group picture. She's angry and so is her mother. They confront you, the person who wrote the cutline, in the newspaper office. What do you say?
- You and others have completed in-depth reporting on student drug use in your school. You've just begun to write the story when the principal gets wind of it. She says you can't publish it because it will reflect badly on the school. Does she have a right to censor the story? What might you say to try to change her mind? Should you have cleared this story with her before you started the reporting or not?
- You're the editor-in-chief and you receive a signed letter from a student objecting to the school's policy on proper attire for the graduation ceremony. You print parts of the letter, omitting parts that refer to the principal in unflattering terms. The student complains of censorship in his next flammable letter. How will you reply in the paper?
- A staff cartoonist submits a rough sketch of an editorial cartoon to accompany an editorial on gossiping. It suggests that girls gossip more than boys. The cartoonist insists that that the cartoon merely depicts the truth and that it's meant to be funny. What do you think? How will you solve the problem?

Responsible Journalism

Professional Ethics: Ask students about the need for certain professions to abide by a code of ethics. Which types of professions should be most subject to penalties for violations of ethics? (Students may mention medical professionals, teachers, lawyers, and police officers.) Why these and not others?

Ethics in Action: Ask students to discuss the ethics of the following situations:

- The paper prints a photograph of a male basketball player crying after the loss of a championship game.
- The paper prints a photograph of a female cheerleader crying after the loss of a championship game.
- During an interview for a profile on new students, the reporter asks whether any of

the students are illegal immigrants.

- In a news story about a 60-year-old teacher who slipped, fell, and broke her hip in the icy school parking lot, she is referred to as "elderly."
- You try to make an appointment to talk to the mayor about the potholes and poor street lighting in front of the school. She doesn't have time to talk, but an aide calls you back and offers to pick you up and talk to you over lunch. He takes you to a hot dog stand and buys you a chili dog and a soft drink, which you accept.
- You interview a student whose first language is not English. You have some trouble understanding a few things he says. Back at the computer, you think he said he was born in South Korea. Or was it North Korea? You settle on South Korea in your story, figuring no one but the student will know the difference and you can always claim it was an honest mistake.
- The math teacher tells you "off the record" that he is thinking of accepting another job for next year. You print what he says in a news brief.
- The school board president said, "There is a severe shortage of science teachers, but we are still looking to add one to the faculty." You quote him as saying, "There is a severe shortage of teachers, but we're still looking for a science teacher."
- You know for a fact that a fellow journalist made up a feature story about cheating on exams. You report this to your adviser.
- You used a joke in your column that you saw on the Internet but did not attribute it.

Assessment

Explore Your World To assess students' understanding of libel, have students explain why the statements they identify are libelous. Tell students that some supermarket tabloids have been sued, so they don't always "get away with" their stories. Assess students' ideas on whether these tabloids should be censored in any way, reminding them of First Amendment freedoms.

Expand Your Skills Determine from students' paragraphs whether they understand state laws concerning freedom of expression.

Express Yourself In addition to the questions in the *Handbook,* ask students whether they think journalists should stick to reporting and spend less time expressing their opinions. Assess how well students have analyzed reasons for whether journalists deserve public criticism.

Chapter 10

Beyond the School Newspaper

Building Background

Tell students that many people become journalists after acquiring expertise in another area. Science reporters, financial reporters, travel writers, writers on religion, and medical writers, for example, all require vast amounts of knowledge beyond journalistic skills, knowledge they may have acquired at a university and from practical experience.

Encourage students to find out about journalism schools, such as the Medill School of Journalism at Northwestern University, and to locate and skim copies of magazines such as *Editor & Publisher,* which deal with topics relevant to journalists.

Journalism Opportunities

Career Day: One way of acquainting students with journalism opportunities is to hold a journalism career day. Students from one or two other schools might be invited as well. Schedule individual presentations and panel discussions involving broadcast and print journalists. Include public relations writers, copy editors, freelance journalists, photographers, webmasters, printers, and graphic designers. Speakers might discuss qualifications for their jobs as well as matters of ethics.

Students can plan, design, and produce a program for the day, and you may be able to get funding for lunch for the participants from the PTA or other service organizations.

Assessment

Explore Your World Students can start by looking around home for printed material. They may be surprised at the number of local people who write, design, and produce newsletters, bulletins, and fliers for clubs, religious groups, and professional, civic, and political organizations. Evaluate their lists of jobs and job tasks and the accompanying journalism skills needed to see whether they have fully investigated possibilities.

Expand Your Skills Students pursuing this assignment might first think of their hobbies or interests. Are they good with animals? expert model builders? Do they have a green thumb? skills at cooking? painting? Do they play an instrument? tutor younger students? All these and other interests could evolve into journalism opportunities. Assess the originality of students' presentations.

Express Yourself Evaluate the appropriateness, organization, content, and tone of students' letters.

Journalism

A Handbook for Journalists

Mark Levin (Author)
Director: National Elementary Schools Press Association (NESPA)
Adviser: newspaper
Carolina Day School
Asheville, NC

Richard P. Johns (Senior Consultant)
Executive Director: Quill and Scroll Society
School of Journalism and Mass Communication
The University of Iowa
Iowa City, IA

Kaye Bird (Reviewer)
Adviser: newspaper
Indiana Junior High School
Indiana, PA

Michele Dunaway (Reviewer)
Co-chairperson: Journalism Education Association (JEA) Middle/Junior High School Commission
Adviser: newspaper and news broadcasts
Rockwood South Middle School
Fenton, MO

Pat S. Graff (Reviewer)
Liaison: Journalism Education Association (JEA)/ National Council of Teachers of English (NCTE)
Adviser: newspaper, radio/TV news broadcasts, and literary magazine
La Cueva High School
Albuquerque, NM

Brian Martinez (Reviewer)
Adviser: newspaper and yearbook
McCullough Junior High School
The Woodlands, TX

Mark Sherwood (Reviewer)
Adviser: yearbook
Milwe Middle School
Longwood, FL

EXp[3]

Journalism

A Handbook for Journalists

Mark Levin

National Textbook Company
a division of NTC/Contemporary Publishing Group
Lincolnwood, Illinois USA

Interior and cover design: Grenier Design Associates
Interior and cover illustrations: Scott Matthews

ISBN (student edition): 0-658-00282-1 (hardbound);
0-8442-2392-1 (softbound)
ISBN (teacher's edition): 0-658-00287-2 (softbound)

The author gratefully acknowledges Ann Lagarde, Carolina Day School, Asheville, NC, for her contribution to the Research Resources information provided in this text.

Published by National Textbook Company,
a division of NTC/Contemporary Publishing Group, Inc.
4255 West Touhy Avenue
Lincolnwood (Chicago), Illinois 60712-1975 U.S.A.

Manufactured in the United States of America.

Library of Congress Cataloging in Publication Data
Levin, Mark, 1952
EXp3— journalism : a handbook for journalists / Mark Levin.
p. cm. — (EXp3)
Includes index.
ISBN 0-8442-2392-1 (SB handbook)
1. Journalism Handbooks, manuals, etc. 2. Journalism Problems, exercises, etc.
I. Title. II. Series
PN4775.L45 1999
070.4—dc21 99-33230
CIP

99 00 01 02 03 04 05 06 07 08 09 QB 0 9 8 7 6 5 4 3 2 1

Contents

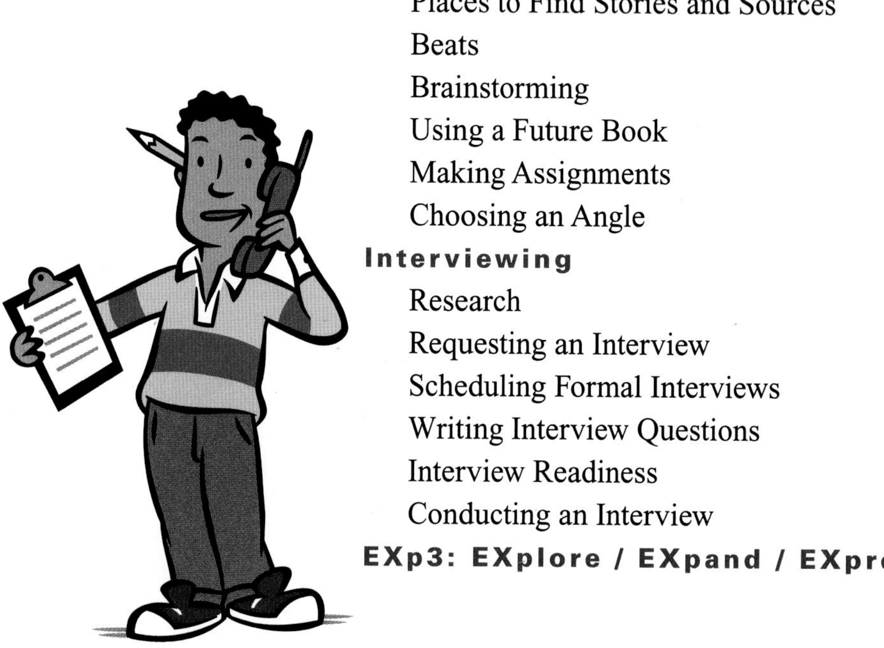

Chapter 3

Chapter 4

Chapter 5

Copyediting and Proofreading 119

Chapter 6

Chapter 7

Photojournalism 173

Chapter 8

Chapter 9

Chapter 10

Introduction

EXp3: Journalism is the first in the *EXp3* series, which focuses on three goals necessary for your success in any field of study:

- **Explore your world** to understand the role of a subject in the world beyond the classroom.
- **Expand your skills** in that subject.
- **Express yourself** with those skills to make an impact on the world.

EXp3: Journalism concentrates on newspaper journalism, but the concepts and skills are applicable to all areas of journalism.

The Handbook

The *EXp3 Handbook* will give you the nuts-and-bolts information you need to become a good journalist. It's designed as a handy reference book. Carry it with you and refer to it often.

It'll prompt you to explore your world as you discover the people, issues, and events that form the news and the way that news is presented to the public. As you do, you'll come to understand the important role played by the media.

It'll provide you with information and techniques so you can expand your skills in journalism: You'll learn how to recognize news and report it responsibly in well-designed newspaper pages. You'll learn to manage tasks and meet deadlines. You'll become a better writer and a more critical reader.

It'll give you opportunities to express yourself. You'll contribute to the efforts of the newspaper team and relish the satisfaction of delivering the news to your readers. And you'll use your skills to express yourself beyond the school newspaper.

Exercises at the end of each chapter will help you use the *Handbook* your first time through it. They're intended to help you fulfill the *EXp3* goals. The *Workbook* provides more in-depth practice on journalism skills.

Press Time

Throughout the *Handbook* you'll be treated to the *Press Time* features, which give you brief bites of journalism history. The expression *press time* refers to the time at which a newspaper is sent to the printer. The news is said to be current "as of press time."

Your Journalist's Notebook

Good journalists carry a notebook with them always. In it they write notes, story ideas, names and addresses, and any other useful information that might help them to cover a story or run the newspaper business.

You can create your own Journalist's Notebook. Any notebook will work, but a three-ring binder is ideal. Fill it with paper and add some dividers. Customize your notebook for your uses.

The word *journalism* comes from the French word *journal,* meaning "daily." Get in the habit of using your notebook on a daily basis. Jot down ideas, practice writing, vent your frustrations, and record your successes.

The Express Yourself exercises at the end of each chapter will offer you further opportunities to use your Journalist's Notebook.

Publishing a Newspaper

The Newspaper Team

Publishing a newspaper may involve a few people or a few hundred people.

Whether the newspaper staff is large or small, everyone must work together to produce a newspaper. Journalism depends on teamwork.

A school newspaper team works amazingly like a professional newspaper team. There's one big difference: On a school paper you'll probably do the jobs of several people. If you decide to become a journalist, you'll have an insider's insight into what each job involves—and you'll have experience!

So who's on the team? Every newspaper is organized in its own way, and the titles assigned for each position vary. Yet the core positions on most school papers have duties that are similar.

Publisher (Adviser)

The **publisher** is the head of the whole operation. In professional newspaper companies the publisher is often the owner. In school journalism the publisher is the school administration. Usually, the school board sets the guidelines for the paper and the principal ensures that they're carried out. But it's the adviser who makes sure the paper gets published.

To do this, the adviser has to train a whole crew of junior journalists as well as oversee what goes into the paper. The adviser also has to see that there's enough money to run the paper.

When there are issues to discuss between the school administration and the newspaper staff, the adviser mediates the discussion. If there are disputes among the staff, the adviser helps settle them.

Advisers don't do what the staff does: write, edit, design, or take photographs. They do, however, offer their opinions and make suggestions.

Editor-in-Chief

The **editor-in-chief** is next in the chain of command. The editor-in-chief makes final content decisions and supervises the entire staff in the overall operation of the paper. Sure, it's a position with prestige and power—but with it comes pressure too.

In exchange for the editor-in-chief's guidance and advice, the rest of the staff needs to be cooperative, supportive, and open. Open communication promotes productive teamwork.

Some papers give the responsibility of day-to-day operations to a **managing editor.** The managing editor serves as vice-president just like the editor-in-chief serves as president.

Press Time

In 1718, when he was 12 years old, Benjamin Franklin was apprenticed to his older brother James. James was publisher of the *New England Courant.* By the time Ben was 23, he was in charge of the *Philadelphia Gazette.* His efforts helped to turn the paper into one of the most successful in the colonies. He went on to found a chain of colonial newspapers—in addition to his achievements in science and government.

Section Editors

Like most newspapers, yours is probably divided into sections such as news, sports, entertainment, and so on. On many papers each section is headed by an editor. A **section editor** is a section expert—someone who knows the section topic inside and out. On some papers, these editors are known as **page editors.**

The section editor's main job is to give reporters story assignments and to work with the reporters to make those stories shine. On school papers, section editors usually serve as reporters too.

Copy Editors

A copy editor checks **copy** before it goes into the pages. Copy is any and all words that will be set in print. The copy editors double-check the copy for accuracy. They also see that it conforms to the newspaper's rules for grammar, punctuation, and word usage.

Professional newspaper staffs may employ several copy editors. On school papers, however, reporters and section editors often serve as their own copy editors.

Reporters

Reporters are the backbone of the newspaper staff. They search out story ideas, gather the facts, and write the stories. It's this simple: No reporters, no newspaper.

Some reporters track down whatever stories they're assigned. These are general-assignment reporters. Others cover a **beat,** which is a particular area of news, such as sports or entertainment.

Reporters that are new on staff, or are just beginning in the field, are known as **cub reporters.** At first, cub reporters may be assigned routine duties in the newsroom. Later, they may try reporting different types of stories.

Design Editor

On school papers, a design editor oversees staff members who serve on the design staff in addition to their other roles. Members of the design staff arrange the stories, photos, illustrations, and ads on the pages and may provide artwork. On some papers, artists who aren't on the newspaper staff contribute artwork as needed.

The design editor makes sure the content appears in a way that's exciting to look at and easy to follow. The design editor may also supervise the **production** of the paper—everything that goes into preparing the pages for the printer or the photocopier.

Photographers

Every newspaper needs photographers. Photos draw readers and add appeal to just about any story.

Photographers usually work on assignment. A section editor may assign a photographer to take a photo for a reporter. Or a reporter may request a photograph. Photographers on school newspapers often serve as reporters themselves.

Some school papers have a photography editor who works with the other editors to coordinate photographs needed for each issue. The photography editor trains and supervises the photographers.

Business Manager

Raising money and keeping track of where it goes are the key duties of the business manager. On a school paper, the business manager works closely with the adviser to manage funds.

Funding for a school newspaper may come from a variety of sources, including advertising. For this reason, the business manager often doubles as the advertising manager. On most school papers, everybody on staff is responsible for selling, writing, and designing ads.

Circulation Manager

The **circulation** of a newspaper is the total number of people and places that receive the paper. The circulation manager coordinates the **distribution**—all methods of getting the paper to the readers. In addition, the circulation manager maintains the **morgue.** The morgue is a collection of back issues of the newspaper, needed for reference and historical record.

On a school newspaper, the circulation manager role is sometimes an add-on to the duties of another staff member. Often, the business manager supervises the circulation manager. The entire staff usually pitches in to help with distribution.

School Newspaper Staff

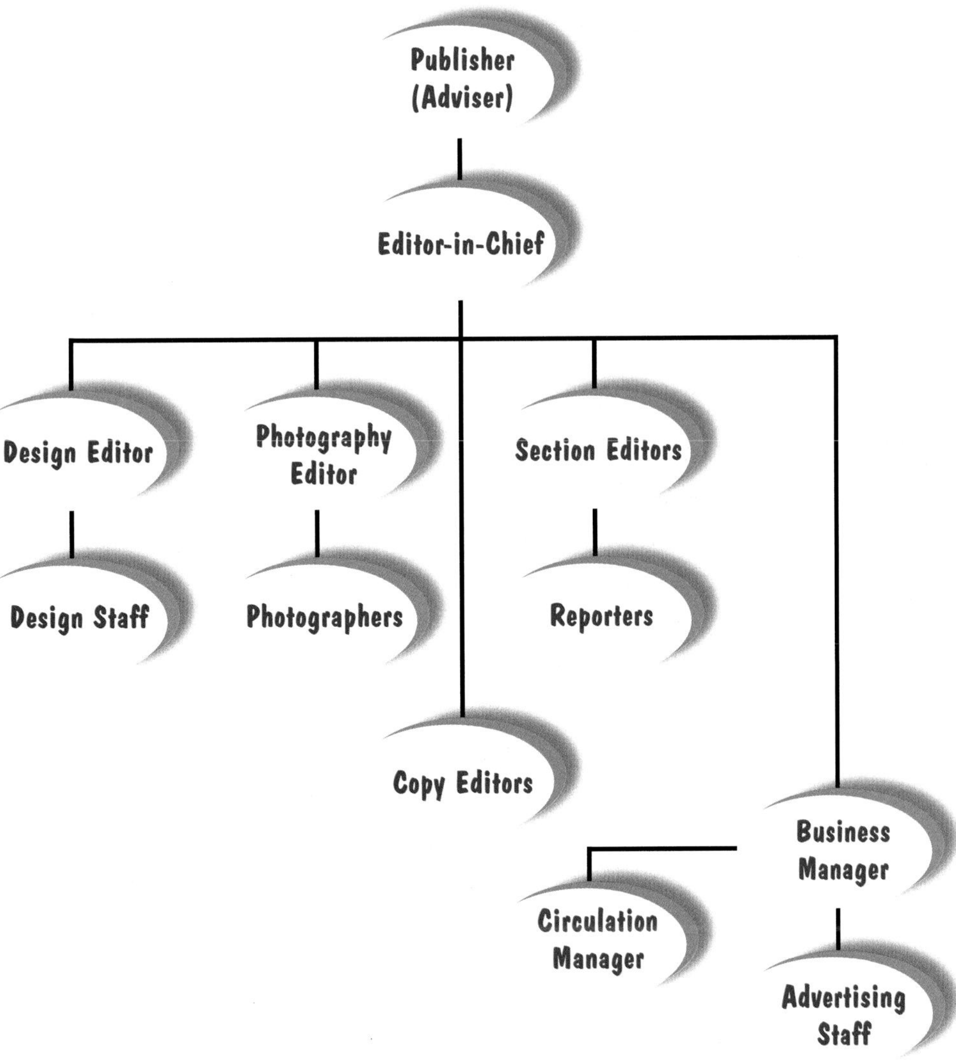

The Readers

Hey, my name's in the paper! Cool. What's this? Hmmm. I didn't know that. What? I don't believe this! Let's see what this says here.

Whatever job (or jobs) you do as part of the newspaper team, keep your readers in mind. They're the ones you're aiming to satisfy. In most schools, the readers include the following:

- students at your school and their families
- teachers, staff, and administration at your school
- your community (local businesses, library patrons, local government officials, and so on)
- journalism students at other schools
- scholastic journalism organizations and press associations

Press Time

The Students Gazette was the first student newspaper published in the United States. It was handwritten by Quaker students at Friends Latin School in Philadelphia—now the William Penn Charter School. The first issue was published June 11, 1777. It proudly proclaimed that it contained "Advices both Foreign and Domestic." The motto read, *"Communi utilitati, consulere debemus,"* which is Latin for "We ought to serve the common good." The school still has a student newspaper: *The Mirror.*

Readers Determine Content

Readers have a tremendous impact on what a newspaper publishes. If readers are satisfied with the content of a paper, they'll keep reading. Circulation will increase. More advertisers will sign on. The paper will grow and improve. If readers are disappointed or disapprove of the content, they'll stop reading. Circulation will drop. Advertisers will pull out. Lack of funds will threaten the paper's future.

How do readers impact your paper? Well, school newspapers do seem to have a built-in audience—the students and their families. Your paper might even be free. But are you sure your audience actually reads and values the paper? If not, you're publishing the paper only for yourselves, and that's journal writing, not journalism.

What Readers Want and Need

To please your readers, give them what they want. This is usually content that's entertaining or interesting. In a school paper this might include tips to ease test anxiety, a review of a new computer game, and a story about how it feels to be a minority.

Journalists also have a duty to offer readers what they need to know or will appreciate knowing. In a school paper this type of content might include stories that inform students about sports team records, school vandalism, and new rules about backpacks in class.

The Editorial Board

Balancing what readers want and need often falls to an **editorial board.** An editorial board for a school paper meets regularly to discuss content and plan future issues of the paper.

Like the boards of professional papers, your editorial board also decides the newspaper's official opinion on issues and makes decisions about the editorial page (p. 109).

A typical editorial board includes the adviser, editor-in-chief, section editors, business manager, and design editor. Sometimes it includes the entire staff.

Readers may think they want "fluff," such as advice columns and horoscopes. Student journalists aren't qualified to offer either, so don't. Gossip is out too. It's legal quicksand. Readers won't miss the fluff if they're offered well-written, meaningful copy.

The Process

Ideas + Action + Paper + Ink = Newspapers

This might seem like a simple equation, but publishing a newspaper isn't simple. It's a business and a craft requiring creative and technical know-how at every step of the process. Whether you're publishing a daily, weekly, bi-weekly, or monthly paper, the process is basically the same.

You'll learn more every day about all the particular tasks involved in the process of publishing your own paper. Watch what others are doing. Ask questions. Volunteer to help out in different areas. Learn the ropes.

Overview of the Process

In general, these are the steps your paper will go through before your readers hold it in their hands:

1. The editorial board meets to discuss the next issue. If they're well-prepared, they've already planned parts of each issue for the entire year.

   They map out a workable deadline schedule: The first deadline is for first drafts of stories. The second is for final drafts and art—photos and illustrations. The third deadline is for designed pages to be checked. The last deadline is for finished pages to go to the printer or the photocopier.

2. The editor-in-chief calls a staff meeting to discuss the next issue. Everybody brainstorms ideas. Content for the issue is finalized. Section editors give reporters and photographers assignments. The design editor gives assignments for illustrations. The business manager makes assignments for ad sales.
3. Reporters start work on their stories. They research the topic, schedule interviews, write interview questions, conduct the interviews, and schedule photographs. Editors guide and assist reporters. At the same time, other staffers are busy selling ads.
4. Reporters write stories. Photographers take and develop pictures. Artists work on illustrations. Everyone submits their work to the editors prior to the first deadline. Editors work with the staff to make any necessary changes. Copy editors check over all copy.

   By this time, ads have been sold. The business manager checks the sales. Editors help refine ad copy.
5. The editor-in-chief and section editors approve final copy. The design editor approves photos and illustrations. Everything is then handed over to the design staff. The design staff prepares the pages under the direction of the design editor.
6. The design editor delivers pages to the editor-in-chief for review. Everyone checks for errors. The design staff makes any necessary corrections.
7. The editor-in-chief approves final pages. Pages are sent to the printer or the photocopier, depending upon the method used for reproduction. Now's the time to celebrate! The paper has been "put to bed" as they say in the newspaper business.
8. If the paper is printed commercially, the printer prepares the pages for the **press,** the machine that prints the paper. When the papers are printed, they're bundled and delivered to the school.

If the paper is photocopied, the pages are copied, bound (usually stapled), and delivered to the school. Some schools may photocopy their papers using school facilities.

9. The circulation manager coordinates distributing the paper to the readers.
10. The adviser and the entire staff read the paper. They critique, or review, the paper. By discussing what did or didn't work they can plan how to improve future issues of the paper.

1 **Explore Your World** Read one page from each section of a professional newspaper tomorrow. Consider how the content of that paper reflects the readers. Who are they? Where do they live? What are their interests? Think about how that paper was put together—the staff involved and the time and skills it took.

2 **Expand Your Skills** Make a list of all the communication and technical skills represented by a newspaper team (for example, the ability to offer specific, helpful criticism and the ability to take qual-ity photographs). Which of those skills do you already possess? Which do you want to sharpen? Which do you want to gain?

3 **Express Yourself** Write a letter to the readers of your school paper. Explain how you think your school paper does or doesn't address what they want and need to read. Describe how you plan to serve them as a student journalist. Include your letter in your Journalist's Notebook.

News Gathering

Defining News

It's a bird! It's a plane! It's a plane painted like a bird. It's landing on your football field. Is it news?

Simply put, **news** is information about events, people, or issues that the public wants or needs to know. Reporters often refer to news as "stories."

Reporters have to be alert and extra sensitive to a good story. In the jargon of journalism, they have to develop a "nose for news." They also have to learn to judge what is and isn't news.

If you hear that a plane painted like a bird is landing on your football field, you may want to check it out. But what if it's just a toy plane? What if it's a model plane that's part of a student's science project? Is it a story your readers want and need to know?

Newsworthiness

When you judge whether something is news, you're determining whether it's **newsworthy.** How can you tell if something is news?

Elements of News

One way to judge whether something is newsworthy is to ask yourself if it contains the **elements of news**—the characteristics of a story that make it appeal to readers. If you answer yes to most of the questions below, you've got news.

Timeliness: Is it current or new?
Human interest: Is it about other people's lives and emotions?
Proximity: Is it happening nearby?
Prominence: Is it well known to your readers?
Consequence: Will it affect your readers in an important way?
Conflict: Does it involve tension, surprise, or suspense?

The "Who Cares?" Test

Another quick way to test if something is news is to ask yourself, "Who cares?" If you think enough of your readers may want or need to know the information, your story is probably newsworthy.

Most students will care about a story if it's about someone they know, about themselves, or about something that matters to them personally.

Press Time

Before 1844 news reports were sent across the country by horseback or railroad. It took days or weeks for reports to reach the newspapers. That year, with the invention of the telegraph, news could be transmitted across great distances in the blink of an eye. Newspapers were suddenly packed with current information from places near and far. During the Civil War readers throughout the nation received detailed accounts of battles the day after they were fought.

Take care when you set out to determine if something is news. Your readers may be interested in something because it's shocking, exciting, disgusting, or unusual, but it may not be newsworthy.

Avoid printing stories that are in bad taste or that result in **sensationalism.** Sensationalism is the tendency to publish information that causes an intense but brief interest or emotional reaction.

Hard News and Soft News

News stories are often divided into two broad categories: **hard news** and **soft news.** Hard news, also called straight news, is strictly factual reporting of news that's current and important. Readers want and need to know hard news as soon as possible. Stories covering the new principal, revisions to math requirements, and theft of sports equipment are examples of hard news.

Soft news entertains as well as informs. It usually appeals to the emotions and is less current and important than hard news. An interview with a student musician, the results of a survey on students' favorite authors, and a movie review are all soft news.

Daily and weekly newspapers offer hard news and soft news. School newspapers publish less often, so most of what they offer is soft news.

Schools can still report hard news, but it's best to look for events in the future and report on issues or plans surrounding such events. When the paper arrives, the news will look fresh. You can also give periodic reports on important issues at your school, such as rising school enrollment or plans to improve computer resources.

Finding Stories and Sources

A news story may be anywhere: hanging out in the locker room, yelling from the bleachers at a wrestling match, or sitting on a bench in the mall.

As you develop your nose for news, you'll find stories almost everywhere you look. They may even find you. Someone may give you a **tip**—information that leads you to a potential story.

Often, you can get a story idea directly from a **source.** A source provides reliable, truthful information on a topic. Sources are not just resources for story ideas. Once you've found a story, you need to locate sources to give you enough useful facts to complete your story.

Types of Sources

A **primary source** offers the best and most reliable information on a topic—information that's essential to your story. Often a primary source is an expert, someone recognized as a leading authority on a topic. Or a primary source may be a person with firsthand information on a topic. A primary source may also be an original document or an official report.

Always find at least one primary source for your story. But don't stop at one. Use as many as you need to tell the story.

A **secondary source** offers reliable second-hand information on a topic. Reference books and other media are common secondary sources. People with informed opinions on a topic can also serve as secondary sources. Use secondary sources to expand your information.

Journalists sometimes quote an **anonymous source** to get "inside" information that the source might not otherwise offer. Generally, however, journalists frown on the use of such sources.

Evaluating Sources

Be choosy about which sources you select to gather facts. Make sure they're up-to-date and have a reputation for accuracy. If you have a doubt about any information from a source, double-check it with another source.

Be especially cautious with Internet sources. Just because it's in print, doesn't mean that it's true. Anyone can publish information on the Internet.

If you gather source material on the Net, use the web sites of well-known newspapers and magazines, government agencies, and high-profile public service organizations. Verify facts on business sites since they may be slanted to favor the business.

Keep in mind that you may need to cite Internet sources in your story. You don't want to cite "Harvey's Happy Homepage." Most people wouldn't consider that a very reliable source. After all, who's Harvey? What are his credentials? Your readers might begin to doubt other sources in your newspaper too.

Places to Find Stories and Sources

To find good stories and sources, you have to be active, curious, imaginative, and self-motivated. Look, listen, and take notes wherever you go, whatever you do.

To start you out, here are the most common places for you to find stories and sources for your school paper.

School: classrooms, hallways, cafeteria, gym, auditorium, library, coaches' offices, guidance offices, school calendar, and administrative offices

Local community: local media (newspapers, magazines, TV, and radio), libraries, museums, city hall, businesses, and community organizations

Global community: national and international media, the Internet, and books

Beats

Your section editor may assign you a beat (p. 4). Look for stories and contact sources on your beat every few days. Talk to adults and students. Consult students of various ages, interests, and backgrounds—and not always the same ones!

Beats for Student Journalists

Beats vary from school to school. Here are some common beats for student journalists.

Academic beat: one or more academic departments (science, language arts, music, math, and others), academic clubs, and extracurricular groups for those departments

Sports beat: one or more official school teams, intramural teams, and sports clubs or groups, as well as coaches, pep or booster clubs, and cheerleaders

Club beat: school clubs that are not academic or sports clubs

Administration beat: principals and superintendents, deans, teacher organizations, school board, and student council

Staff beat: guidance counselors, librarians, janitors, cafeteria workers, and other adults who are not administrators or faculty

Community beat: community events and organizations with high student interest, parent-teacher organizations and activities, and corporate-sponsored school programs

Brainstorming:

Some of the best ideas for stories and sources arise during a brainstorm with your newspaper staff. For the most productive results, it's best to organize the brainstorming. Follow these steps:

1. Appoint a leader and someone to record the ideas.
2. Have everyone think for a few minutes, and then jot down ideas.
3. In a given order, have the leader call for each person to state an idea in one or two sentences. No criticism of ideas is allowed. Have the recorder write down each idea on a chalkboard. Repeat this step for more ideas.
4. Vote to rank the ideas in order of interest and importance.
5. Discuss top-ranking ideas further if necessary.
6. Make decisions about which stories to cover.
7. Make story assignments.

Using a Future Book

A **future book** is a listing of events, by date, that you may want to cover in future issues of your paper. Only one future book is necessary for your school paper, although you may want to make your own.

Good resources for your future book include tips (p. 19), newspaper clippings, flyers or posters in the community, and events calendars from your school, park district, and community arts organizations.

TIPS Using a Future Book

- Use a binder filled with empty pages, separated by dividers for each month of the school year.
- Add to your newspaper's future book once a week. When you add tips, include the source of the tip. When you add clippings, make sure each is labeled with the publication and date.
- Include all the information you have about the event, such as names, dates, times, phone numbers, addresses, and descriptions of the event.
- Next to each entry, jot down ideas for stories about these events.
- Refer to your future book when you plan each issue.

Press Time

Benjamin Day stirred up the world of news with his New York daily paper *The Sun*. Founded in 1833, it was the first successful "penny paper." The paper's content focused on human-interest stories from the police and the courts as well as other local news. The price of one penny and the mass appeal of its content contributed greatly to its popularity. In 1835 *The Sun* reported that the moon was inhabited by "bat-like creatures." This sensational hoax helped drive the newspaper's sales up to 19,000 copies daily.

Making Assignments

Once the stories and potential sources have been identified, it's time to make the assignments. An editor may assign a story on the basis of a reporter's abilities, interest, or both. Beat reporters are often assigned stories on their own beats. But this doesn't mean they can't cover other areas as well.

Organizing Assignments

Since an average student newspaper may include as many as 20–30 stories, a story might slip through the cracks unless you're well organized. Record the assignments. Display the information where the entire staff can refer to it easily and frequently.

A chalkboard or other erasable board makes a good assignment board; you may need to change or update information.

Arrange the information simply. You might use a chart. Everyone should see at a glance who's assigned to do what.

Include the following information:

- the story assignment
- the reporter and editor assigned to the story
- the photographer assigned, if any
- the design staff person or artists assigned, if any

Keep stories in each section together. Allow space to indicate completion of tasks. You may also wish to leave space to show the status of the story—where it stands in the process of putting together the issue.

Choosing an Angle

The approach you take to a story is your **angle.** An angle is usually different from the typical approach to a story that others may take.

Bear in mind that there's no *correct* angle for a story. For a story on the spring musical, you might report what goes on during a typical rehearsal or what the tech crews do during a performance. Has this musical been done at your school before? That could be an angle too.

Try to decide on an angle as soon as possible so you can pin down sources you need. If you don't know what angle to take, you may first brainstorm possibilities. Do your news gathering for those possibilities. Based on what you find, choose an angle.

Often the angle emerges naturally during the news gathering process. Don't be afraid to change angles if a better one appears.

Local Angle

If your story is about an event or issue that originated in another place, try to incorporate a **local angle.** A local angle is someone or something that connects the topic of your story to your local readers.

Including a local angle is called **localizing** a story. You can localize any story by involving real people from your school and community who have a personal tie to a story topic. A story on a conflict in another part of the world, for example, could be localized by interviewing students who have relatives in that area.

Interviewing

The interview is essential to most stories. It's the chewy center in the candy, the sparkle in the gem, the fuel in the engine.

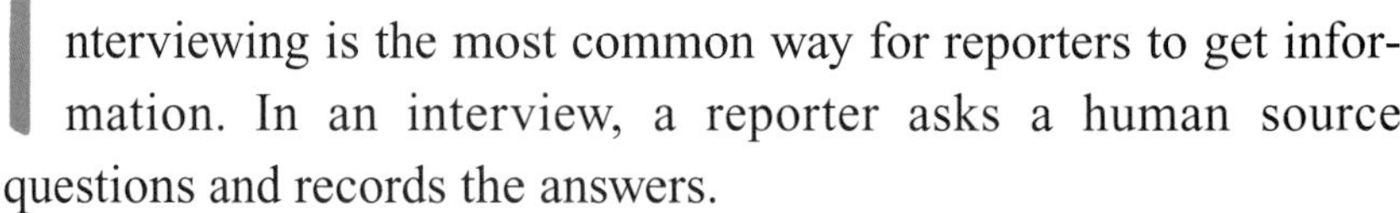

Interviewing is the most common way for reporters to get information. In an interview, a reporter asks a human source questions and records the answers.

Reporters may conduct brief, informal interviews with people they meet casually at events or with people offering on-the-spot information. Other interviews may be formal and in-depth. For interviews with primary sources, reporters usually schedule time for a formal interview and prepare a list of questions to ask.

Many stories simply can't be reported without consulting human sources. Knowing the proper way to prepare for, schedule, and conduct interviews is vital for covering these stories.

Research

Informal and formal interviews usually call for background research on the topic of your story. By doing research to answer general questions, you can save the really good questions for your interview. As part of your research, read related stories in your school paper and in other media. When you cover controversial issues, read information that presents varying viewpoints.

For a formal interview, research the person you plan to interview. If you're interviewing someone who is well known regionally, nationally, or internationally, check your library for the following resources to find information about that person:

- biographical dictionaries
- corporate reports
- almanacs and encyclopedias
- current news articles
- Internet (make sure the source is reliable)

If you're interviewing someone who isn't well known, try consulting these resources about that person:

- friends and family of the person
- co-workers or classmates of the person
- articles in the local media about organizations or activities in which the person is involved
- people who may hold opposing views on information this person can give you

Requesting an Interview

Whether you're conducting an informal or a formal interview, introduce yourself to your source and explain your reason for wanting an interview.

Give the following information:

- your first and last name
- the name of your school and newspaper
- the topic of your story

If you're requesting an informal, on-the-spot interview, don't just dive into your questions. First ask if the source has time to answer a few questions. Be gracious if your chosen source declines your request. Move on to try someone else.

Interview Modes

Do your interviewing in person whenever possible. A face-to-face interview allows you to interact naturally with your source.

Some reporters conduct interviews over the phone or on the Internet using e-mail or a chat mode. These methods, however, offer no opportunity to observe your subject.

Perhaps your source can only grant a phone or Internet interview. Conduct a phone interview in a quiet, private place. Position yourself so you don't have to juggle your notebook and the phone. Speak slowly and clearly when you ask questions. For e-mail or chat-mode interviews, get a printout of the interview.

Scheduling Formal Interviews

One of the most important interactions you have with a primary source may be the first one, when you request a formal interview. Approach your sources in an organized, professional way. Show that you respect their time and expertise. They'll be more willing to work with you—on this story and perhaps later on other stories.

TIPS Scheduling Formal Interviews

- Make arrangements to meet at a time and place that's convenient (and safe) for your source and for yourself. Don't interfere with the source's other prior commitments, including class work.
- Choose a quiet place where you can talk freely and privately.
- Have several time and location options worked out so you can make suggestions.
- Block out at least 20 minutes of time (more if you have lots of questions). Arrange for another half hour if you need to have photos taken.

- Keep your deadline in mind as you schedule your interview. It takes time to set up an interview with someone who's busy.
- If you plan to use a tape recorder in the interview, ask if your source has any objections.

Writing Interview Questions

Good stories come from good questions. Write and refine your questions before interviewing. Take time to make them effective.

At the very least, you'll need to write questions that answer the journalist's main questions: *who, what, when, where, why,* and *how.* These are known as the **5 W's and H.**

For an informal interview, you may write only a few questions. For a formal interview, be prepared with about 10–15 questions.

TIPS Writing Interview Questions

- Stay focused. Write a statement of purpose for your interview.
- Write questions that aim to answer the 5 W's and H.
- Write questions that are simple, clear, and get right to the point.
- Write **open-ended questions.** An open-ended question is one that allows the source a wide scope in answering. It's a question that can't be answered by one word, such as *yes* or *no.*
- Write questions to make your source think. If you can predict an answer, it's probably not a good question.
- Write questions that seek the truth, even if the truth may be sensitive or embarrassing—but phrase such questions politely.
- Write questions that get at what your readers want to know.
- Write questions that reveal how the topic relates to your readers.

Interview Readiness

Being a reporter means that you have to be ready for an interview at any time. You never know when you may run across a story. And of course, it's vital that you be prepared for scheduled interviews.

TIPS Interview Readiness

- Take your basic tools—notebook and writing utensils—wherever you go. You may want to carry them in a backpack to protect them from weather.
- If you use a tape recorder, test it frequently. Always take notes anyway, just in case.
- Include extra paper, pencils, and pens in your supplies. Include extra batteries and blank tapes if you use a tape recorder.
- Group questions in categories that proceed in a logical sequence.
- Write prepared questions in a notebook. Leave space after each question to write the answers.
- Allow space after a prepared question for **follow-up questions** and the answers to those. A follow-up question is intended to get a source to further explain or expand upon a previous answer.
- Leave space in the margins to jot down notes on body language. Such observations can add visual depth to a story.
- Write your questions on one side of a page and number your pages. You'll be glad you did when you organize your notes.
- Be ready to drop prepared questions and ask new ones. (Don't forget to write these new questions as well as the answers.)

Conducting an Interview

During an interview, you have to get accurate and complete information, interact in a polite but relaxed manner with your source—and often do it within a time limit! Reporters and sources alike can be nervous under such conditions.

Take a deep breath. Remember that you're conducting the interview. You're setting the pace and leading the way.

Opening the Interview

- Open by introducing yourself. Thank your source for taking time for the interview. Set up and test your tape recorder if you're using one. Be friendly. Chat with your source while setting up.
- Announce the purpose of your interview to your source. Then ask your questions in the order in which you have arranged them.

During the Interview

- Throughout the interview, listen carefully. If you don't understand something, ask your source to explain it again or in a different way.
- Let your source know you're listening. Nod to show you understand. You may wish to summarize each answer before moving to the next question, allowing your source to add or correct information.
- Take notes while you listen—even if you're tape-recording. Develop a legible note-taking language to help you take notes faster.
- Be conversational, but let the source do most of the talking.
- Never supply or suggest an answer. Be patient and wait for it.
- Underline or place a checkmark next to all names, numbers, words, or ideas you're unsure of so you can check them.
- Don't interrupt a source unless it's unavoidable. Then simply raise your index finger to say "wait." Allow your source to complete his or her thought before continuing.
- Listen for well-turned phrases and powerful or lively sentences that would make good quotes. Take time to get the exact words. Read the quote aloud from your notes to make sure it's correct.

Closing the Interview

- When you've covered all of your questions, ask the source if he or she has anything to add. At this time, you may also ask if your source recommends any additional sources for your story.
- Before closing the interview, look over your notes. Check spellings, numbers, and other details with your source.

- Close by thanking your source. Ask permission to contact him or her again to verify information if necessary. Get your source's address so you can send a copy of the printed story.

After the Interview

- Immediately after the interview, try to list the main points of the story. At the same time, jot down any ideas you have for how you'll write the story and what you think are the highlights.
- As soon as possible after the interview, rewrite your notes so they make sense to you. Use your tape recording to help fill in gaps. Contact your source again to supply missing information or to check what remains confusing.

Sometimes a source will refuse to talk about a topic. Or the source will only discuss the topic if it's off the record. *Off the record* is the term used to explain a particular type of agreement between a source and a reporter. The agreement may be that the reporter will not print off-the-record information that the source provides. Or the agreement may be that the reporter will not name the source of the information if printed.

In general, it's best to avoid any information a source may give you if it's prefaced with statements such as "This is off the record . . . ," "Don't quote me . . . ," or "I shouldn't be telling you this but . . . ."

1 **Explore Your World** Read a story in a local or city paper. Imagine how the reporter may have found the story and the sources. Think about the questions the reporter asked to get the information in the story.

2 **Expand Your Skills** Listen carefully the next time a friend or family member starts to tell you a story about an event, person, or issue. Practice being a reporter. Determine if the story is newsworthy. When you find someone with a newsworthy story, interview that source to get more information. When you've finished the interview, organize your notes and identify the main points.

3 **Express Yourself** In your Journalist's Notebook, write about an experience you've had in an interview situation—either as a reporter or as a source. If you've never been in an interview, write your thoughts about the interview process as you imagine it will be for you as a reporter.

Journalistic Writing

FAMOUS QUOTES
THESAURUS
DICTIONARY

Qualities of Journalistic Writing

"Journalists cannot march in the parade. They can only stand on the curb and write about what goes past and why."

—Roger Mudd, award-winning TV journalist

Journalism offers a wide variety of writing experiences. But every journalist gets started by learning the basics of journalistic writing. Journalistic writing focuses on reporting the facts of a news story—the *who, what, when, where, why,* and *how.*

Joseph Pulitzer, a reporter and publisher of the 1800s, stressed one of the most important qualities of journalistic writing in his memorable command, "Accuracy! Accuracy! Accuracy!" Roger Mudd's quote above refers to another important quality: objectivity.

In addition to accuracy and objectivity, all journalistic writing should be clear, concise, and colorful. If your writing exhibits these qualities, you're bound for success.

Accurate Reporting

Nothing is more embarrassing and unprofessional than writing a story that has factual inaccuracies. Someone *will* notice, and you'll hear about it. As a reporter, you're responsible for the information printed in *your* story. Don't leave it to your editor to catch errors. Review everything carefully. Your reputation, and that of your newspaper, is at stake.

TIPS Accurate Reporting

- Verify each fact and quote against your notes. If you're in doubt about anything, check with your sources again.
- Double-check the spellings of student, faculty, and staff names, as well as grades and titles. Refer to official documents listing this information, such as homeroom lists or a school directory. You can get these from your school office.
- Keep a current phone book and an atlas handy to double-check the names of organizations and places.
- Double-check dates, using a calendar.

Press Time

Hungarian-born Joseph Pulitzer was editor and publisher of the *St. Louis Post-Dispatch* and the *New York World* during the 1800s. He popularized a new form of journalism. It was a mix of sensationalism and aggressive crusading for political and social reform. To provide an incentive for excellence in journalism, Pulitzer established the Pulitzer Prizes. He also founded the Columbia School of Journalism in New York City, one of the first university schools devoted to training journalists.

Objective Reporting

Journalistic writing calls for strict objectivity from a reporter. To be objective you must report the facts without bias—without including your opinions or letting them slant the reporting.

Understanding the difference between facts and opinions is vital for objective reporting. A fact is something that can be proven to be true. An opinion is a personal viewpoint open to dispute.

Your sources will likely provide you with opinions as well as facts. An interesting story contains both. *Your* opinion, however, has no place in the story. The exception is some types of soft news, such as opinion pieces, where readers expect to hear a writer's personal views (p. 102).

When you include your opinion in journalistic writing, you're **editorializing.** If you report about a school pep rally and write that everyone had a great time, you're editorializing. You can't prove that everyone had a great time. Report what you saw and heard, not what you think or feel. Let the readers draw their own conclusions.

Balance

To be objective, you must also be balanced. Most stories have more than one side—even those that seem straightforward. A student council decision, for example, might be the result of a battle between two or more sides on an issue.

Controversial topics always have at least two sides: A new curfew law for minors or a banned book is sure to stir up many differing opinions.

Present all significant viewpoints of a story. But be careful as you choose which sources to draw from and which opinions and facts to use. Give equal time to pro and con views. Whether or not you intend to, you can tip the balance of a story.

Strive for a thorough, fair representation of all sides. You have an obligation to report not only the truth but the whole truth.

TIPS Objective Reporting

- Cite the source of all opinions in your story.
- If you're unsure whether you're editorializing, ask yourself, "Would *everyone* agree that this is true?"
- Eliminate the words *I, me, my, mine, we, us, our, you,* and *your* from your story unless you indicate that someone else said them.
- Avoid any words that suggest a judgment or opinion—such as *should, good, excellent, cool, poorly, unfortunately, hopefully,* and *especially*—unless you make it clear to readers that someone else said them.
- To help maintain balance in each issue, make a list of sources cited. On an official list of students, faculty, and staff, place a check mark next to the name of each person whose opinion you cite in a story. Avoid quoting a person more than once during the school year unless that person is a vital source for your story.
- Don't quote your friends. Readers will make the connection and can very quickly decide the reporting is not balanced.

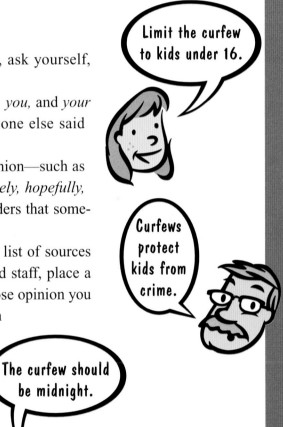

Limit the curfew to kids under 16.
Curfews protect kids from crime.
The curfew should be midnight.

Clear, Concise, and Colorful Writing

Journalistic writing must be clear and concise, or readers won't take the time to read it. Worse yet, they may not understand it. Journalistic writing must also be colorful, or readers won't enjoy reading it.

The best way to be clear is to be simple. Simple writing isn't dull writing. Striving for simplicity can lead you to be more careful as you compose your words. This usually results in crisp language that brings the facts of a story to life.

Concise writing is economical writing. Get to the main facts quickly. Leave out information that doesn't help move your story forward. And don't waste words. If 10 words say it, why use 20?

That doesn't mean all descriptive words should be left out. Just use them when they have impact. When you do use description, choose vivid nouns and verbs to create pictures in the minds of your readers. That's colorful writing.

Paragraphing and Transitions

Good journalistic writing flows in a smooth, logical sequence. Each paragraph should have no more than one main idea. Make that idea clear to the reader in the first sentence of the paragraph.

For better readability, keep your paragraphs short (40 words maximum). But don't make them all short. Vary the length to add rhythm to your writing.

To link ideas within and between paragraphs, use **transitions.** A transition is a device that helps the reader follow the story. Think of transitions as signs that remind readers what the story is about and direct them to where the story is going.

Transitions may be key words, phrases, or ideas that are repeated from previous sentences or paragraphs. These include synonyms of key words, such as *dog* for *poodle.* (Synonyms are words with nearly the same meaning.) Synonyms can also be the pronouns *he, she, it,* and *they,* and the adjectives *these, those, that,* and *this* if they refer to someone or something.

Other transitions are words or phrases that direct the thought sequence. These include words that show time *(then, later, meanwhile),* words that point out contrasts *(but, however, instead),* words that lead to conclusions *(therefore, thus, so),* and words that cite examples *(for example, for instance).*

TIPS Clear, Concise, and Colorful Writing

- Choose simple words over "big" words. For example, choose *saw* rather than *visualized, huge* rather than *gargantuan.*
- Be precise in your word choice. Did the coach *scream* or *shout?*
- Avoid slang and **jargon** (technical or specialized language).
- Avoid **clichés** (trite, overused words or expressions).

If you want your writing to be light as a feather, bite the bullet and avoid clichés like the plague. Everyone will think you're smart as a whip.
CLICHE
CLICHE

- Use strong, specific nouns and verbs (*granite* rather than *rock, stroll* rather than *walk*) instead of strings of descriptive words.
- Recast sentences that start with boring verb constructions, such as *there is/was/are, this is/was,* and *it is/was.*
- Be direct. Use the active voice instead of the passive voice. State *who* did *what,* not *what* was done *by whom.* For example, write "Cage drove the car," not "The car was driven by Cage."
- Avoid long sentences. Try to keep them to about 15–20 words. Some sentences may be very short for rhythm and variety.
- Use short paragraphs. Two or three sentences each is about right. Shoot for no more than 40 words per paragraph.
- Avoid wordiness: "With two seconds to spare, Lee made the winning basket" is better than "With two seconds remaining on the clock, Lee took the shot, resulting in the winning basket."
- Eliminate redundancies, such as "3 p.m. in the afternoon," "continued on," and "the color red."
- Read your story aloud to another staff member to see if it flows smoothly and logically. Listen to that person's comments and add paragraph breaks and transitions where you need them.

Press Time

Newspapers in the Old West sometimes took the idea of colorful writing to the extreme. Writers often stretched the truth, or even invented it, for the sake of entertainment. This sometimes led to misunderstandings. One fabricated story described a strange magnetic phenomenon in the Pahranagat Valley of Nevada that caused rocks to move toward each other. The story caught the attention of a group of scientists who were studying electromagnetism. They contacted the paper and demanded further details of the discovery.

Writing Leads

You can lead readers to a story, but you can't make them read—unless you've got a fascinating lead.

The **lead** is the beginning of your story. It *leads* readers into a story. A lead can be as short as one sentence or as long as four or five sentences. Typically one paragraph, it can be two or three.

Whatever the length, your lead must be well written, appropriate to your angle (p. 25), and interesting. In many cases, it's all readers read. If you want them to continue beyond the lead, you've got to grab their attention right at the start.

Easier said than done. Even seasoned journalists find leads challenging. Many leads are tried and many discarded before the perfect one is chosen. Nevertheless, writing leads is rewarding. You'll know when you've got a good one—and so will your readers.

Summary Lead

The most traditional lead is the **summary lead.** A summary lead is to the point and factual. It's meant to give the reader a quick summary of the story in as few words as possible, usually in one sentence.

Here's a typical summary lead:

> The purchase of new school buses will strain next year's budget, school board president Anita Barr announced at the March 18 board meeting.

Summary leads often focus first on the *who* and *what* of the story and then follow closely with the *when* and *where.* The *how* and *why* may be explained or suggested further into the story.

To write a good summary lead, follow these guidelines:

- Use few words (no more than 30 words, preferably fewer).
- Focus on the most important of the 5 W's and H (p. 29).
- Summarize the most newsworthy fact within the first 10 words.
- Begin with the subject of the most newsworthy fact (usually the *who* or *what*).
- Clearly identify any named person (by title, grade, and so on).
- Cite the source of any opinions.
- Set the appropriate tone for the story—light or serious.

Creative Leads

Unless you're writing hard news in a daily newspaper, the summary lead just doesn't reel in readers. Leads for stories in a school newspaper generally require more creativity.

Here's an example of a creative lead on a story that could have been given a standard summary lead:

> Not even subzero temperatures could stop progress. With a thud, bulldozers churned the icy earth, beginning work on the new performance center.
>
> "The performance center will offer students state-of-the-art facilities and relieve overcrowding of current spaces," Superintendent Jean Maples said at the groundbreaking ceremony last week.

When you use a creative lead, it may not contain the most important facts or tell exactly what the story is about right up front. That information may be delayed until a later paragraph, which journalists call the **nut graph.** It's the paragraph that contains the basic core—or nut—of the story.

Don't take too long getting to the nut graph. Try to hit it by the third paragraph at the latest. In the example below, the nut graph is the second paragraph.

> "Clones! Or am I seeing double? Hey, are you guys related?"
>
> Teenage twins Megan and Margo Feldman, 10th grade, say dealing with "lame" jokes is just one of the disadvantages of going through life as a twin. But they admit there are plenty of advantages too.

Variations of Creative Leads

Some reporters use established variations of creative leads. Just make sure they suit your story and your angle (p. 25). And don't use more than one of each type in the same section of your paper.

Scenic Lead: Begin with a description of the scene surrounding an event. This lead is typically used for stories in which the setting is prominent, such as stories about carnivals, dances, and other festive events. It can also be used to strike a mood appropriate for the story.

> Bubbles floated through sea-green streamers. Turquoise light played on the walls. Sea shells cupped glimmering candles. With the first notes of "Atlantis," the Under-the-Sea dance began.

Storytelling Lead: Using a narrative style, begin by introducing the main characters, the conflict, and perhaps the setting of the story. Make readers feel the drama and want to know what's going to happen next. Identification of people can be postponed until a later paragraph to avoid disrupting the narrative flow of the lead.

> The man reached out a dirty hand, palm up.
>
> "All I've got is a few bucks," Jim Rae said, reaching into his pocket.
>
> The next thing Rae knew, he was on the ground with a boot on his chest. Rae, a 6th-grader, was being mugged.

Punch Lead: Open with an amazing fact or a startling statement that arouses reader interest.

> Eastmont cooks serve nearly 500 pounds of pasta each week for lunch.

Opposite Lead: Cite first one point of view or observation and then follow with the opposite view.

> TV rots the brain, according to a report by child psychologist Julie Bower. Heidi Eliot, 8th-grade genius, says that just isn't true.

Blind Lead: Unless names or locations are extremely well known *and* of high interest, begin with the interesting fact and lead the reader into the following paragraphs to get the specifics.

> For saving the life of a victim of a hit-and-run car accident, two 7th-graders were honored for bravery.
>
> In a ceremony held last week, Jay Inman and Paul Elk each received a plaque naming them heroes. Inman and Elk pulled seven-year-old Ken Kijama from a car just before it exploded.

Avoid using a question or a quote as your lead. These are overused and misused lead variations.

Open with a question only when it's compelling and is the focus of the story. Never use a question lead as a conversational opener, such as "Have you ever wondered . . . ?"

Open with a quote only if it's a unique, fascinating statement that can stand on its own. Take heed: Such statements are rare.

Another common crutch is to start a lead with "Picture this . . ." or "Imagine . . . ." Readers have seen this too many times. Don't do it.

Writing Captivating Leads

Writing a lead that's a natural beginning for your story *and* that captivates readers isn't easy. But it can be fun. Keep in mind the qualities of journalistic writing and put forth your best effort.

TIPS Writing Captivating Leads

- Make your lead introduce your angle (p. 25).
- Make it appropriate to the tone of your story—light or serious.
- Consider using *why* and *how* leads instead of *who* and *what* leads. A *why* lead concentrates on the cause or reason behind the news. A *how* lead explains the way something happened.
- Avoid *when* leads, unless the time something occurred is by far the most important fact. Too many stories start with a dull accounting of time, such as "This year, . . . ," "On Oct. 4, . . . ," or "Last week, ..."
- Avoid starting with a reference to your school or a school group.
- Create a question in the reader's mind—without actually asking a question.
- Avoid stating the obvious—for example, "Winter is here again."
- Never use a dictionary definition. It's the lazy way out.
- Use strong verbs! Above all, avoid starting your lead with those oh-so-blah verb constructions: *There is/was/are, It is/was, This is/was.*
- Don't settle for the first lead you come up with. Try several before choosing the best one.

Handling Quotes

"Our job is not to make up anyone's mind, but to open minds."

—Fred W. Friendly, former president of CBS News

A quotation, or **quote,** is the exact wording of a statement from a source. The statement may be a fact or an opinion.

Quotes are essential to all stories. They add human interest and expand on the content.

Quotes also make a story more believable. Readers are more likely to trust the truthfulness of information if they know it came from a source other than the reporter.

As a reporter, you need to understand the types of quotes and how to handle them correctly.

Direct Quotes

Quotes printed exactly, word for word, are **direct quotes.** The words of the quote appear within quotation marks with the **attribution** outside them. The attribution is the phrase that tells the source of the information—where or from whom you got it.

Direct quotes are used when a source expresses an opinion. This is an example of a direct quote:

> "I couldn't have done it without the director," said Lauren Salm, 11th grade, who played Juliet.

You must use the exact wording when you quote directly. Even one word left out or changed can alter the meaning:

> "I could have done it without the director," said Lauren Salm, 11th grade, who played Juliet.

When you change the words or meaning of a quote, you're **misquoting.** Frequent misquotes will erode the good reputation of your newspaper and can lead to legal problems.

Indirect Quotes

When you include information from a source without using the source's exact words, you're using an **indirect quote.** An indirect quote is a paraphrase, a summary of the meaning of the direct quote, reworded by the reporter.

Use indirect quotes in the following situations:

- when you want to express a fact stated by a source
- when a direct quote is too long, confusing, or dull
- when you want to condense the ideas of several direct quotes

Attribution of indirect quotes differs from attribution of direct quotes. In most cases, if the information is a fact, no attribution is necessary. If it's an opinion or a controversial fact (one that people may question), attribute it. The paraphrase includes the attribution. No quotation marks are necessary.

Here's an example of an indirect quote that expresses an opinion, so it's attributed:

> Chris Nye, 10th grade, said he sees graffiti on some of the walls around town, but said he doesn't know what any of it means.

Take care not to misquote. You run a high risk of misquoting when you paraphrase because you interpret what a source said.

Partial Quotes

Reporters sometimes select key words or revealing phrases from a direct quote to include within an indirect quote. Like a direct quote, the exact wording in a **partial quote** must be contained within quotation marks. The attribution is part of the indirect quote.

Use partial quotes when you need or want to use a source's exact words but the direct quote is too long or confusing. A partial quote is especially useful for highlighting lively or memorable words, especially those that express an opinion.

This is an example of a partial quote:

> Jenna Ward, 11th grade, said that tattoos are a "tribal thing" that unites her with others of her generation.

The danger of misquoting exists with partial quotes as with the other types of quotes. You're transplanting words. Perform the operation carefully.

Using Quotes Correctly

The many rules for using quotes correctly are simple once you know them. Take time to learn them thoroughly.

Attribution Verbs

Attributions generally use verbs phrased in the past tense. The word *said* is the most common and all-around best verb for attributions.

You may be tempted to use synonyms for *said.* Resist the temptation. Other verbs are suitable only in specific situations. Follow these rules when you're in doubt:

- Use *asked* when the source asked a question.
- Use *added* only when a source added information to a statement just made.
- Use *stated* only when a source read from a prepared text at a speech or press conference.
- Use *according to* only when you're quoting from a printed source that announced conclusions of a report or study.
- Use verbs such as *yelled* or *whispered* only when you're using a direct quote in which the source definitely did yell or whisper.
- Never use a verb that indicates a movement other than speaking, such as *shrugged* or *smiled.* You can't shrug or smile a word.

Where and How to Attribute

- In general, place the attribution verb after the source and any standard identification, such as title or grade:

  "I love roses," Laura Duffy, guidance counselor, said.

- If you want to tell a bit about the source besides just the name and the title or grade, place the attribution verb before the source:

  "My yard is overflowing with flowers," said Duffy, who gardens as a hobby.

- If the information in the quote is more important than the source, attribute after the quote:

  "This school is run down," Kurt Chang, 6th grade, said.

- If the source is prominent, attribute before the quote on the first reference:

  Tipton mayor Barb Gomez said, "School renovation is on our list of critical issues to address next year."

- For direct quotes of multiple sentences, attribute after the first sentence:

  "My bulldog is cool," Tim Volk, 8th grade, said. "He has these sloppy jowls. I laugh every time I look at him."

Punctuating Quotes

- Put all exactly worded quotes within quotation marks.
- Place the end punctuation of quotes within the quotation marks:

  "Why can't teens vote?" Ryan Hawk, 11th grade, asked.

- Use only one punctuation mark at the end of a direct quote:

  "What a day!" Carrie Graham, 10th grade, said.

- When the attribution comes after a direct quote, use a comma instead of the end punctuation (unless the end punctuation is a question mark or an exclamation mark):

  "Teachers should get paid more than doctors and lawyers," Bart Kelly, 7th grade, said.

- When the attribution comes before the direct quote, place a comma after the attribution verb:

  Benjamin Franklin said, "There is no little enemy."

- If a question mark relates to the sentence and not the quote, place it at the end of the sentence outside the quotation marks:

  Who said, "I shall return"?

- Use single quotation marks to indicate a quote within a quote:

  "My favorite songs are 'Robot' and 'Crow,'" Dalton Weis, 12th grade, said.

- Begin a new paragraph each time the subject matter of a direct quote changes and each time you quote a different source:

  "Hobby Shop is for anyone with any hobby," Gina Hernandez, 8th grade, said. "I'm into watercolor painting."

  Bill Coyote, 7th grade, makes model airplanes. He said he enjoys the way students in the Hobby Shop club share tools and teach each other different skills.

- Leave off the closing quotation marks at the end of a paragraph if the quote continues into the next paragraph:

  "We're planning a trip to Rowan Observatory," Sufi Chowdhry, science teacher, said. "It'll be open to students who complete all assignments on time.

  "Funding for the trip will be raised by private donations," she explained. "We already have a donation from Handy Construction."

- Don't break a subject from its verb with an attribution, this way:

  "Life," Fran Leibowitz said, "is something that happens when you can't get to sleep."

- If a quote is a complete sentence, begin it with a capital letter. If it's a fragment, don't:

  He lives by the proverb "Live and let live."

  Principal Jackson warned students to "get serious."

Using Quotes

- Attribute all opinions.
- Attribute facts only when they're controversial.
- Use a variety of direct, indirect, and partial quotes.
- Don't use quotes to repeat information already in the story.
- Don't use quotes that state the obvious.
- Use direct quotes early in the story to spark reader interest.
- If direct quotes are boring, make them indirect or partial quotes.
- Quote your primary source most often (p. 19). Incorporate a balance of quotes from secondary sources as necessary.
- Leave out profanity and meaningless words such as *um, uh,* and *you know* in direct quotes from a speaker. You can also make minor corrections in grammar to prevent a speaker from sounding uneducated.
- To clarify a confusing or strange word or phrase within a direct quote, insert a translation within brackets.
- Add the word *sic* ("thus") in italics within brackets after words that are misspelled or used wrongly in a direct quote from a printed source. This indicates the quote is exactly as in the original.
- Check potentially offensive or misleading quotes with your editor, adviser, and even the source, before including them.
- In addition to taking written notes during an interview, tape-record it so you can verify quotes later.
- Never use the phrase "when asked" or "in response to a question about" to lead into a quote.

Organizing the Story

The three bears lived happily ever after once upon a time before Goldilocks ate all the porridge and broke Baby Bear's chair.

Organizing the way you tell your news story is as important as organizing the way you tell any story. Readers won't tolerate a confusing story. They want a story that reads clearly and naturally.

In journalistic writing, the first step to writing an organized story is to organize your interview and research notes so they make sense to you. Only then can you begin to organize the story so it makes sense to your reader.

As you prepare for this task, be on guard against a common blunder: organizing your story in the order in which you took your notes. It's very unlikely that you clearly and naturally organized the elements of your story during your news gathering.

Getting Ready to Write

Good reporters try to write their stories as soon as possible after an interview. You may feel exhausted, but it's best to get going while the information is fresh in your mind.

Before you sit down to write, follow these steps to organize your notes and your thoughts:

1. Rewrite your interview and research notes so they're complete and make sense to you.
2. Categorize the information in your notes under each of the 5 W's and H or under other topic headings that emerge.
3. Prioritize. Which facts are most newsworthy? Which quotes are most interesting? You may find it helpful to number your facts in order of importance and put stars next to interesting quotes.
4. Which quotes correspond to which facts? Match them up.
5. Write a statement of one or two sentences that explains the story. Imagine you're telling a friend about it. This statement will guide you as you write your lead and the rest of your story. Make sure your statement explains your angle (p. 25).

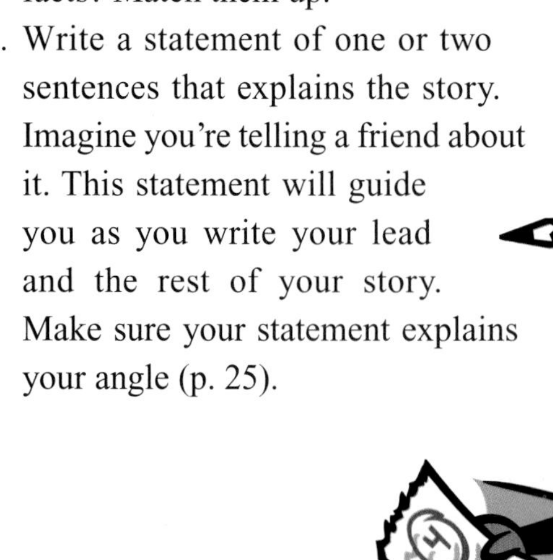

Press Time

In 1892 a *Chicago Globe* editor told cub reporter Theodore Dreiser (who later became a famous novelist) that the first paragraph of a story must reveal "Who or what? How? When? And where?" This inverted-pyramid format first began to emerge after the advent of the telegraph in 1844. Telegraph transmission was expensive, and the lines were sometimes unreliable. Reporters therefore sent only the most newsworthy facts in short, paragraph-long dispatches. The dispatches were used as the lead paragraph, and details were filled in afterward.

The Inverted-Pyramid Format

News stories, especially hard news, are traditionally written in the **inverted-pyramid** format. In this format, the most important information comes first. In each successive paragraph, the information is a little less important.

Stories are written this way for two main reasons: If readers don't have time to read the whole story, they'll get the essential information right up front. And if an editor has to shorten a story to fit the space, it's easier to whack a few paragraphs off the bottom (while keeping any closing paragraph) instead of carefully going through and trimming the whole thing.

Of course, reporters hate having a story cut for any reason. That's just part of the life of a newspaper reporter.

No formula exists for writing an inverted-pyramid story, but the diagram on page 60 may help you organize stories in which you use this style.

The Inverted-Pyramid Format

Lead

This will usually be a summary lead. If it's a creative lead, get to the nut graph right away.

Additional Information

If the lead doesn't contain all the important facts, add them here. Weave in quotes that support and explain the important information. Work down to what can be left out.

Background Information

Add what isn't necessary. This may be something that helps put the story in perspective, such as a comparison to a similar news item.

Closing

Wrap things up. You may refer to information in the lead or finish with a direct quote that sums up or helps balance the story.

The Storytelling Format

In the **storytelling format** you report the news but you do it in a story. You set the scene, introduce the characters, and narrate the events, weaving in facts and opinions from your sources.

If the news item is an event, describe the people and the actions in each part of the event. Work from start to finish or begin at the end and tell how things came to that end. If possible, focus on just a few main characters, incorporating their comments on the action.

If you're using this format to write about a person, tell a story (or a series of short stories) that reveal what the person is like. For example, what led the new principal to a career in education? Describe experiences. And include details, which make good storytelling.

If your story revolves around an issue, tell a story about people affected by the issue. For a story on the dangers of smoking, you might focus on a nurse who treats lung cancer patients or tell how a teenager began smoking, learned to hate it, and successfully quit.

The Q & A Format

Q: What's a Q & A format?

A: It's a format for a story that shows both the questions and the answers of an interview (just like the format here).

Q: When do you use it?

A: The Q & A format is used only for soft news. It's an interesting way to present an interview that focuses on a source's opinions or personal history.

You can also use the Q & A format to explain an unfamiliar concept in a simple way. The questions serve as topic guides.

Q: How else does the Q & A format differ from other organizations for stories?

A: Unlike stories organized in an inverted-pyramid format, stories that use the Q & A format aren't likely to have a priority order of important information. Yet some questions and answers are bound to be more interesting than others. You can put those first, but it's more important to make sure the ideas in the story flow naturally from one to the next and make sense to the reader.

Q: Can you use this format in a school newspaper?

A: Sure. Readers like it—in small doses. But don't use the Q &A format unless you plan it first with your editor.

Sidebars

During news gathering, you often find interesting, useful information that doesn't quite fit your angle. You may decide you'd like to present it with your main story somehow. You can do this by using a **sidebar.**

A sidebar is a story that's closely related to, or adds to, the main story, or **mainbar.** A sidebar typically runs to the side of the mainbar. It's often boxed or set off in some other obvious way. A sidebar is always shorter and less important than the mainbar. It should never repeat information in the mainbar.

A mainbar may have more than one sidebar. For a story on the upcoming state golf championships, for example, you might have a sidebar that explains several golfing superstitions. In addition, you might have one about the way a golf green is groomed.

Sidebars add not only information to your paper but visual interest as well. Readers are drawn to pages that include short stories.

Quick-Read Menus

A **quick-read menu** is a type of sidebar that offers a brief, well-organized selection of specialized information. Like other sidebars, it's set off from the mainbar and is less important.

The following are common types of quick-read menus:

Quote collection: quotes on the topic of the story by students, faculty, and staff, or by famous people

Fast facts: The 5 W's and H of the story broken down into precise points of information

Bio brief: a short profile of a person or organization cited in the story, listing key characteristics relevant to the story

List: a series of facts, names, statistics, and so on that add depth and context to the story

Glossary: a list of terms with definitions that help readers better understand the story

Checklist: a list of questions or guidelines that prompt readers to itemize key points or assess needs referred to in the story

Time line: a chronological list of important events in the history of a key person, organization, place, or issue in the story

Step-by-step guide: an explanation of each step in a complex process mentioned in the story

Quiz: a series of questions that let readers interact with the story

Resource reference: a list of resources where readers can learn more about topics addressed in the story

Contact information: a list noting phone and fax numbers, mailing addresses, e-mail addresses, and web sites of organizations mentioned in the story

Writing Headlines

Step right up, folks, and read this story! Yes sir, you won't be sorry you did.

Trying to get the attention of readers is like trying to catch the eyes and ears of a passing crowd at a carnival.

Readers skim newspapers looking for what interests them. They don't want to look hard or get lost trying to find their way.

That's why newspapers need **headlines.** A headline is a very brief description of the contents of a story printed in larger type, usually above the story. The headline calls to readers, tells them what the story is about, and guides them to it.

Headline Construction

Headlines are constructed to vary somewhat in appearance: small, large, short, long, one-line, two-line, set on top of the story, set down in the story.

Headline Style

Newspapers adopt one of two styles of headlines, which they then use throughout every issue. The two choices are as follows:

upstyle: a style of headline in which every major word is capitalized. This is an old style, not used much anymore.

Tigers Crush Spartans in Finals

downstyle: a style of headline in which only the first letter of the first word and proper nouns are capitalized.

Tigers crush Spartans in finals

Headline Formats

The following are several common options for headline formatting:

kicker: a word or brief phrase, set over a longer, main headline

Ups and overs and downs
Pole vaulting cut from track and field

hammerhead: a word or brief phrase set in large, bold type over a longer, lighter main headline

ZAP IT
Microwave meals nourish students on the go

tripod: a two-part headline that consists of a word or brief phrase set in large, bold type alongside a two-line headline that equals the first part in height

Poof: Costly school supplies disappear overnight

Banner: a bold headline that runs the entire width of the page

Janitor hits jackpot

Headline Size

The size of your headline is a signal to readers: The bigger the headline, the more important the story. With your editor, judge the importance of the story.

Some newspapers define a specific headline hierarchy, or order of importance. A number may be assigned to each rank, with each rank designated a specific size.

Editors make the final decision on headline size. Your editor may decide your story is of medium importance, so your headline may be ranked "3" in a range of five levels. That means its size would be within a specified midrange.

Making Headlines Fit

The style, format, and size of your headline go far in determining how much space it takes up. (The other major factor is the font. See p. 152). The design staff will allow space for your headline on the pages as they plan where everything goes. You'll write a headline to fit the space, in the size specified by your editor.

The Telegram Method

Like a lead, a headline must capture and hold a reader's attention. And like a summary lead, it must summarize the story. Because of greater space limitations, however, it must do so in far fewer words—like a telegram.

A telegram is a brief, often urgent message sent via a message service to someone who's difficult to reach. The message is delivered by phone or by hand-delivered letter within one day. Telegrams are priced according to the number of words used, so people use the fewest words possible.

Try this headline-writing method, known as the **telegram method,** which is used by many headline writers:

1. Read your entire story. As you do, jot down words or phrases that indicate main points of the story.
2. Use your notes to write a one-sentence summary of the story. Imagine you're sending the summary to a friend in a telegram.
3. Trim your telegram by cutting out all the unnecessary words. Use key words only.
4. Try to trim it even further. Apply the rules of headline grammar and punctuation on the next page and you've got a working headline. You may have to revise it a bit, but you've got a start.

TELEGRAM
STUDENT SHOWS IN LOCAL GALLERY

Headline Grammar and Punctuation

- Include an active verb in every headline.
- Use the present tense of the verb for past actions:
  Skateboarders clash with police
- Use an infinitive for future actions:
  Bus drivers to strike for higher wages
- Tell what was done, rather than what was not done.
- Use figures for numbers. Ten and under may be spelled out.
- Avoid separating hyphenated words, abbreviations, and parts of a name or a verb from one line of a headline to the next.
- Omit *a, an,* and *the.*
- Avoid forms of the verb *to be,* such as *is, are,* and *will be.*
- Use no more than one abbreviation. Clarify it in the lead.
- Replace double quotation marks with single ones.
- Use a comma instead of the word *and.*
- Never end a single-sentence headline with a period. Use a semi-colon to separate two sentences in a headline.
- Choose one style—and use it for every headline in every issue.

Press Time

The *Chicago Tribune* ran one of the most famous newspaper headlines of the 20th century. During the 1948 presidential election Thomas E. Dewey appeared to have the edge over his competitor Harry S. Truman. The *Tribune* went to press with a headline reading "Dewey Defeats Truman" before the results were in. When Truman was officially declared the victor, the *Tribune* staff raced to recall the papers that had already been shipped out. Thousands of papers were retrieved, but many had already reached the public.

Writing Polished Headlines

Polish your headline-writing skills by volunteering to write headlines whenever they need to be done.

As you write, keep in mind the qualities of journalistic writing and the rules of grammar and punctuation. In addition, take the tips offered here.

TIPS Writing Polished Headlines

- For hard news, summarize the key point of the story only.
- For soft news, be creative, but let the reader know what the story is about.
- Make your headline specific to your story. It should fit no other.
- Write a headline that fits the tone of the story—light or serious.
- Use short, strong, active verbs in your headlines:
  Astronomy club peers into future
- Make sure your headline reflects the importance of the story.
- Never exaggerate or mislead readers just to get their attention.
- Use a banner headline only for really big news:
  Skokie Park District voted best in nation
- Don't use people's names in your headline unless they're very well known. Instead, use a synonym:
  Teacher publishes novel
- Avoid puns and alliteration (repeating the first letter in several words) for hard news. This type of word play can come off as flippant or insensitive:
  Student bounces back after basketball injury

Writing Cutlines

A picture is worth a thousand words—but sometimes a photograph needs a few more words just to make things clear.

A **cutline,** or **caption,** is the information that accompanies a photograph. Newspaper journalists prefer the term *cutline,* while magazine and yearbook journalists use *caption.*

Some people distinguish between the two terms on the basis of placement and length of text: A cutline is the brief text below a photograph or other graphic (p. 137). A caption is a short paragraph next to a photograph that tells a story about it.

Whether you call them cutlines or captions, you need to understand their function.

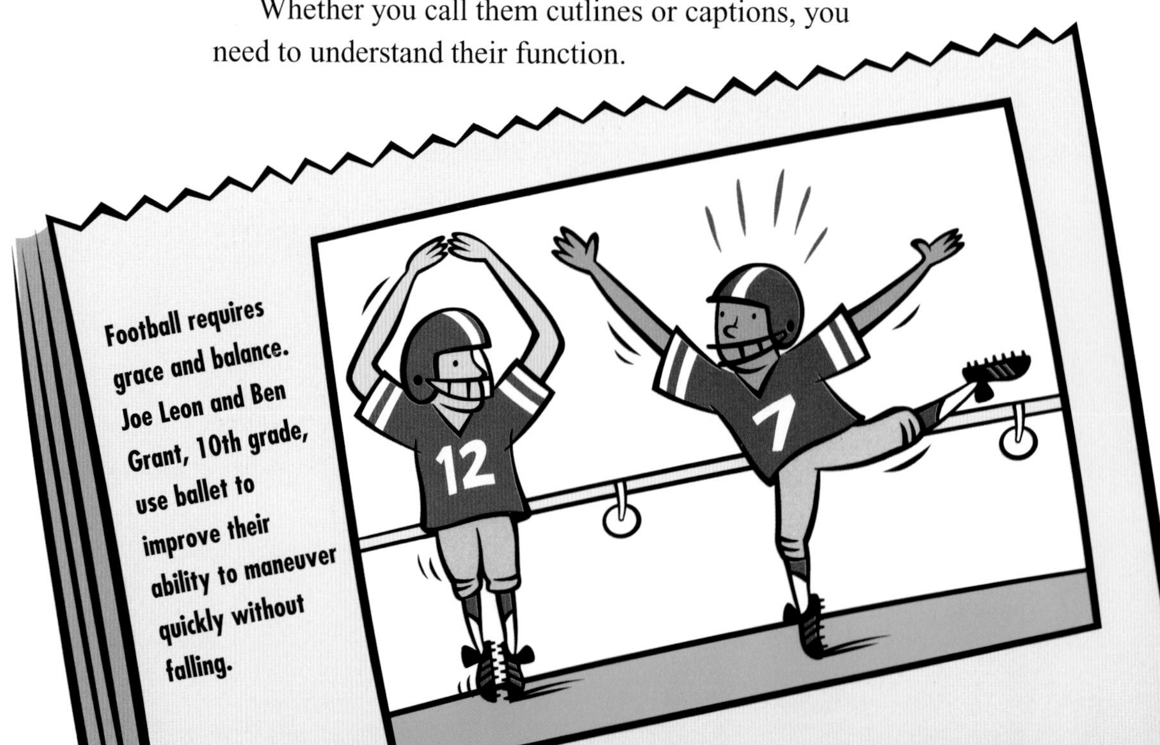

Football requires grace and balance. Joe Leon and Ben Grant, 10th grade, use ballet to improve their ability to maneuver quickly without falling.
12
7

Functions of Cutlines

Cutlines may seem small and insignificant, but they're very meaningful for readers who enjoy photographs. Some readers read only cutlines. A well-written cutline may draw readers into stories.

A cutline fulfills a dual function: It *interprets* the photograph for the readers if what's happening is not apparent. And it may *identify* people, places, objects, or events.

Story Cutlines

Most photographs accompany stories. On occasion, however, a newspaper runs a photograph that stands as a story in itself. The photo and cutline combine to tell the whole story, but the burden falls most heavily on the cutline. It must serve as a ministory, providing the reader with newsworthy facts.

Photo Essay Cutlines

Some photographs are part of a **photo essay.** A photo essay typically consists of three to seven photos centered around an event or a theme. The photo essay may tell a developing story.

The essay includes one or more cutlines. You may write and position a cutline next to each photo. Or you may write one long cutline that refers to each photo in turn.

Writing Meaningful Cutlines

Like all other writing in your paper, your cutline should exhibit all the qualities of journalistic writing. But first things first: You can't even begin to write a cutline without the correct information.

Gathering Cutline Information

Photographers can't just go around snapping pictures. They have to gather information about the subjects of the photographs they take at the time they take the photographs.

Gathering information generally includes getting the accurate full name and title or grade of each person in the photo. For group photos it's best to record names in a left-to-right order for each row, bottom to top. You may want to include a brief description of each person next to his or her name. Subjects sometimes switch places for one or more of the photographs you take.

You should also record information about the place where you took each photo. If it's not evident in the photo, you'll probably identify the location in the cutline.

Analyzing the Photograph

Before you begin to write, analyze the photograph. Jot down notes that answer these questions:

- What information does the photograph give (in particular, how does it answer any of the 5 W's and H)?
- What is its purpose? to inform? to strike a mood? to make readers laugh? to make them feel sympathy?
- What does it symbolize, if anything?

Next, determine what information is obvious from the photograph and what may need to be interpreted or identified. These are the types of items that often call for explanation:

- specific action in a complicated sports scene
- action in an event unfamiliar to most readers
- setting of the photograph
- identification of people and unfamiliar objects

Writing the Cutline

If you're writing a cutline for a photograph that shows only a person's head and shoulders, it may consist of just one line identifying the person by name. Most cutlines run from two to four lines.

Some cutlines are set with the first few words in boldface or all caps to get readers' attention. Keep this in mind as you write your cutline. You'll want those highlighted words to be especially interesting.

When you give any information about activity in the photograph, use the present tense: "Gasket repair on a 1996 Dodge Colt gets greasy for auto mechanics students." Change to past or future tense, as appropriate, when you give background information: "The class has worked on domestic autos this quarter and will concentrate on imports next quarter."

TIPS Writing Meaningful Cutlines

- Don't state the obvious.
- Use strong, active verbs.
- Avoid starting with names unless the focus is on a notable person.
- Don't begin with "Pictured above . . . " or "Here, ..."
- Avoid starting too many cutlines with "ing" verbs.
- Identify individuals in group photos by rows, front to back or bottom to top, not as row 1, 2, 3, and so on. Readers already assume the order is left to right.
- Make cutlines a fairly consistent length throughout your newspaper.
- Add a quote to the end of your cutline to give readers the sense of being there. Use quotes with feeling and opinion, not those that state the obvious or repeat facts in other parts of the cutline.

EXplore / EXpand / EXpress

1 **Explore Your World** Skim a daily newspaper. As you do, place check marks next to headlines that catch your eye. If you read the lead of the story, mark it with a star. If you read the entire story, circle the star. Place an *X* next to cutlines you read.

What made you read a particular headline? lead? story? cutline? Was the writing in each clear, concise, and colorful? How many of the stories you read had summary leads, and how many had creative leads? What was the ratio of direct to indirect quotes? facts to opinions? Did you notice any editorializing? Which headline formats did you see? Did the cutlines perform their dual function?

2 **Expand Your Skills** Read an entire story in a newspaper. Now, try to rewrite the lead, using either a summary lead or a creative lead. If you use a creative lead, don't forget the nut graph. Then write a new headline that you think will fit the space.

3 **Express Yourself** Think about a special event in your life—a prize you won, a move to a new home, the death of a pet. Imagine that you are a reporter, *not* yourself. As an objective reporter, write about the event as if it were a news story. Include relevant facts. Quote yourself directly or indirectly about the event. Use whatever lead or story organization works best for your topic and angle. Write a headline for the story. If you have a photograph that documents the event, write a cutline for the photo. Include your story, as well as the photo and cutline, in your Journalist's Notebook.

Types of Journalistic Writing

News

Two main factors affect news coverage in school papers: time and space. Given the time between deadline and distribution, which stories can you cover? Given the space you have, how broad can your coverage be?

Like many newspapers, your deadlines don't allow you to cover breaking news—hard news that's happening the same day your paper is published. So you cover news that will happen soon or that has happened recently.

A story that covers an event in the near future is called an **advance story.** A story that covers an event in the recent past is called a **coverage story.** A coverage story that follows up on a previously reported story is a **follow-up story.**

In school newspapers, news receives less coverage than other types of stories. Less space might mean less news coverage. You can, however, cover news in ways that let you address a broad range of events.

News Coverage

One way to provide broad coverage for events in your school and community is with **news briefs.** A news brief is a short, condensed news story. It may be a few sentences or a few paragraphs.

Group news briefs together on your news page under a heading identifying them as news briefs. Give each brief a headline. You may opt for a label headline that just states the topic. Just be consistent with your style from issue to issue.

Like other news in your paper, your news briefs will be advance or coverage stories. Group advance stories together and coverage stories together.

News Briefs

French Club to honor faculty
The French Club will honor faculty with a breakfast March 2, 7–9 a.m., in the faculty lounge. French pastries and beverages will be served in a French café atmosphere.

Community theatre auditions announced
Limelight Community Theatre will hold auditions for *Our Town* by Thornton Wilder March 5 at 6 p.m. The play has roles for a teenage female and male. Call 555-343-1244 for details.

Dance raises funds for AHA
The Kind Hearts Dance, sponsored by Student Council, raised nearly $2,000 for the American Heart Association (AHA). Each student who made a donation to AHA received a Kind Hearts sticker and a glowing red pen.

Roving Reporter

Some school papers use a device called a **roving reporter** to cover a wide range of news items. It's essentially a series of one- or two-sentence news reports. Each report is separated by an elipsis (...). A roving reporter is similar in effect to an electronic bulletin board that displays a running line of information.

Beat reporters (p. 4) often find interesting items to put in a roving reporter. These news items might not warrant a story but are worth mentioning.

You can run the reports together as one long paragraph or break them into paragraphs that cover different grades or types of news items, such as clubs, community, and awards. Some roving reporters boldface student names as well as other items that will draw interest. List the events in chronological order from past to present, with upcoming events included last.

Roving Reporter

SmartThrob for October was **Cleo Goia,** 7th grade....**The LMS marching band** played for the Hoover Elementary School Halloween parade on Oct. 27....Eighth-grade technology students finished construction on a miniature **magnetic-levitation train** track Nov. 5....Third-period art classes have their **Seasonal Sculptures** on display in the West Lobby....Forensics competitor **Gwendolyn Duncan,** 7th grade, will go on to a state meet Nov. 18. Her speech topic is home ecology.... Tickets for the Dec. 15 **Holidaze Dance** will go on sale Nov. 20. Tickets are $5 each....

School Calendar

Most schools issue calendars that list dates of holidays, final exams, and sports events. As a service, some school newspapers publish a calendar of upcoming school events—events on the calendar and those recently scheduled.

Present the information in a boxed chart or a list rather than a calendar to save space. Record the date first, followed by the event on the same line. Cite one event per line. Limit coverage to no more than a month in advance, or it gets too overwhelming. And make sure your calendar is concurrent with the newspaper's delivery date.

Since there are so many sports events, you may want to have a separate calendar for those. Place it on your sports page.

School Calendar

11/2	Parents Day
11/3	Activity Night, 6–8 p.m.
11/5	Vision Screening
11/8	Study Lab Opens
11/10–11	Semester Exams
11/12	1st Semester ends
11/15	Spanish Class Fiesta, 2 p.m.
11/15–19	Mini-Courses Week
11/19	Spirit Contest, 3 p.m.
11/20	Founder's Dance
11/22	2nd Semester begins
11/24–29	Thanksgiving Break
12/1	Holiday Food Drive begins

Student Achievement Stories

One of the most common news stories in school papers focuses on the achievement of a number of students. These students may be award winners, members of a sports or academic team, or the cast and crew of a play.

If the event that the students are involved in is newsworthy, write a story about it. But don't include a list of names in the story—unless the number of names is very few (five or less). Instead, list them as a quick-read menu (p. 63). Give the list a simple label headline, such as "Geography Contest Winners."

If the story isn't much more than the list of names, print the list instead of a story. Include a brief introduction if necessary.

When you list student names, organize them properly:

- Cite one name per line. Include the grade after the name.
- For awards, list the most important awards and winners first.
- For a sports team roster, list by grade, highest to lowest.
- Within one grade, list in alphabetical order.

Press Time

Nellie Bly, pen name for Elizabeth Cochran, pioneered investigative journalism in the 1800s—a time when few women were accepted in any field of journalism. One daring assignment was to have herself committed to an insane asylum to expose its horrors. Her reports were front-page news. Bly is also noted for being the first female war correspondent, sending reports from the front lines of World War I.

In-Depth Reporting

Hard news typically concentrates on the *who, what, when,* and *where* of a story. Newspapers increasingly offer more stories that explain the *how* and *why* of a story. Reporting that goes deep beneath the surface of a topic is **in-depth reporting.**

Stories reported in depth are longer than regular news stories. They require extensive research, many interviews, and dozens of sources. No slackers need apply for in-depth reporting.

In-depth reporting on a school newspaper allows you to explain complicated topics. The topic may be related to a recent news item. Or it may be a topic that's "hot" with your readers.

Making It Significant and Stimulating

Make your in-depth story meaningful, or significant, to readers. Perhaps the most important factor in writing a significant in-depth story is finding a unique, localized angle (p. 25) on your topic.

To engage readers throughout an in-depth story, include a wide range of stimulating facts and opinions. Many in-depth stories have accompanying sidebars (p. 62). These invite readers, and highlight interesting aspects of the topic.

Planning In-Depth Coverage

In-depth coverage of a topic requires extra time. Some school papers plan months in advance. Give yourself ample time. And don't procrastinate. A rushed in-depth story will be shallow.

A typical plan calls for one reporter to handle the longer, main story. Other reporters do sidebars related to that story. A photographer and illustrator may be assigned as well. The editor-in-chief or a section editor oversees the coverage.

TIPS In-Depth Reporting

- Focus your topic. For example, narrow the topic of families to cover views on blended families *or* extended families, not both.
- Don't publish an in-depth story that isn't ready. Plan regular status checks. That way you'll be prepared if you need to run other stories instead.
- Use more primary sources than secondary sources.
- Include at least two primary sources for each main point.
- Communicate regularly with others working on the in-depth coverage. Make sure you aren't including the same information in your main story and in the sidebars.
- Give your in-depth story prime space in your newspaper. Front page or in the center of your paper are both good locations.

Investigative Reporting

In-depth reporting that seeks to uncover and expose something hidden is **investigative reporting.** Often what is hidden is illegal. Or it has been purposefully hidden to keep the public from questioning the details.

Investigative reporting by school newspapers typically consists of exposing information about how money and power is used in the school system. Many public school records are open to you and may yield interesting information for in-depth stories. You might find out, for example, that the budget for one program was cut to replace funds for a program that was mismanaged.

A school investigative reporter can also investigate topics that affect the community in general. For example, you might investigate public places where poor street lighting poses a threat at night. You could then report what's being done about it.

You may find that some sources are reluctant to talk about controversial subjects. Take special care with any "off the record" information (p. 33). You may also be denied access to documents you have a right to examine. Work with your adviser and editor-in-chief to ensure that your rights are protected and that you follow your school's policies.

Surveys

Readers like to find out what others think about a topic. A **survey,** or **poll,** helps fill this niche of news reporting. A survey is a report of what people in a specific group feel or think about a topic.

Results are tallied on the basis of the group's responses to one or more questions. A survey story reports percentages of the group that respond one way or another to the question(s).

Random Sampling

Results of a survey can be misleading if the survey isn't conducted scientifically. To be scientific, you must survey a **random sample** of the group. This means that each person in the group must have an equal chance of being polled.

To be representative, your random sample should also accurately reflect different ages, sexes, and ethnic or racial groups. That kind of accuracy is difficult to accomplish in a school newspaper poll.

To ensure a random sample that's *fairly* accurate, follow this general rule: Poll 10 percent of your group or 50 people, whichever is more. You can poll 10 percent by choosing every tenth person on a class list for each grade in the poll. No substitutions are allowed.

Survey Questions

Survey questions should be easy to understand, easy to answer, and easy to summarize or compute. Before you do any survey, test your questions on a small group. Revise them until they work.

You can ask open-ended questions (p. 29), which allow a wide range of responses. Or you can ask **closed questions,** which allow only one answer. Closed questions are *yes*-or-*no* questions or multiple-choice questions.

Answers to open-ended questions provide interesting quotes for a survey story, but they're difficult to summarize into results. They're generally used in written surveys, or **questionnaires.**

Answers to closed questions are easy to count and organize into results. Closed questions are ideal for quick, in-person polls.

You may need to ask **filter questions** to filter out answers that won't be meaningful. Let's say you want to find out whether rap-music listeners think rap-music lyrics encourage violence. You first have to ask the filter question, "Do you listen to rap music?"

Presenting Survey Results

Results of a survey may be published as a story in themselves or as a sidebar to another story. Many results lend themselves to presentation in graphs or charts. Poll results may lead to an in-depth story that explores the meaning or impact of the results.

yes 20% 48%

4 out of 5 no

Consumer Reporting

Cost. Safety. Service. Performance. Quality. These are the watchwords of **consumer reporting.** Consumer reporting covers good and bad buys in the marketplace. A consumer report offers readers factual conclusions about a product or service. The report is based on complete and unbiased news gathering.

Sources for consumer reports should include people who use the products profiled or have experience with them. Sources must also include experts. *Consumer Reports* magazine and other media that specialize in analyzing products are valuable sources.

Approaches to Consumer Reporting

Your approach may depend on the product or service you're covering. These are the most common approaches:

Compare and contrast: Report reasons for differences in cost, quality of performance and service, and safety (if appropriate). You might, for example, compare buying products from local retailers to buying the same products via the Internet. Make recommendations based on the information.

Bargain hunt: Inform readers about where to get the best deals on popular items. Who sells school supplies for the lowest price? Which movie theater is the best all-around bargain?

Consumer advocate: Help solve a consumer problem. What can you do if a store won't take back or replace a faulty product? Report how to cut through red tape to get problems solved. Make sure you research and present the laws surrounding consumer rights. Consumers under 18 years old sometimes have special rights. In addition, your local Better Business Bureau can provide you with any history of complaints about particular companies.

Features

You go whitewater rafting and then write a story about how to ride rapids. You interview a 14-year-old math whiz and report on the teenager inside the genius. You discover that your town was named after a mule and write a humorous account of how that happened.

That's **feature** writing. It's fun writing. But because it's journalistic writing, it's also hard work.

Features are soft news. Like all news reporting, features require you to gather facts and opinions through research and interviews. You must demonstrate the qualities of journalistic writing in your stories, headlines, and cutlines. And most of all, you must satisfy your readers.

The Nature of Features

Most reporters enjoy writing features. Generally, they give more freedom to writers than hard news. Specifically, here's how features differ from hard news and what defines them as features.

Unlimited Range of Topics

As a feature writer, you have the world at your fingertips. If you can think of it, you can write about it: ethnic pride, strict parents, computer hacking, home schooling, retro hairstyles, whatever.

The important thing is to make the topic relevant to your readers. This doesn't mean it can't be something they've never heard about. You just need to find a way to relate it to their world.

Human Interest

You may recall that human interest is one of the elements that can make a story newsworthy (p. 17). Feature writers dig beneath the facts to bring readers the human side of the news. Many features can make readers feel as if they're part of the story. These are the stories that affect readers most dramatically.

Timeliness and Timelessness

Unlike hard news, features don't have to be timely. If they focus on something in the distant past, however, they're usually tied to a recent news item. The way a feature story "hangs" on a related news item is its **news peg.** Features may be advance or coverage stories, hung on a news peg in the future or the past.

Many features are "evergreen," which means they can be used at any time. Timeless features give writers liberty from tight deadlines. They can take a bit longer to explore complex topics, consult a variety of sources, and polish their stories. The stories must be up-to-date, however, when they're published.

Flexibility in Format

Feature writers can be flexible in choosing a format. But all well-written features have a clear beginning, middle, and end.

Features typically begin with a creative lead rather than a summary lead. And they're rarely written in the inverted-pyramid format (p. 59). Studies show that readers prefer the storytelling (p. 61) format for most features.

Mood and Tone

Features can bring smiles, tears, or both to the reader. You can make readers feel the thrill of peering into a volcano or the anger of having possessions stolen.

Press Time

Many journalists—such as Mark Twain, Charles Dickens, and Jack London—have made the transition from reporter to fiction writer. One journalist who has made the transition in recent years is Elizabeth Wong. In the 1980s she was a reporter for both the *San Diego Tribune* and the *Hartford Courant*. Wong has written many plays and television screenplays. Her first play, *Letters to a Student Revolutionary*, was based on her exchange with a Chinese student involved in the 1989 demonstrations at Tiananmen Square.

As a feature writer, you might write to evoke a mood and tone suitable to the topic. You might write to arouse certain feelings in readers. If you tell the story naturally, however, the people and events of the story itself will do the job for you.

Anecdotes, Incidents, and Quotes

Feature writers describe incidents and provide examples to illustrate an idea or prove a point. They incorporate **anecdotes** for the same purpose. An anecdote is a ministory, a short account of an interesting, powerful, or humorous event.

Quotes are used readily in features as well. Many feature writers even use dialogue to add drama to a story. Quotes are also used in hard news, but they're used to answer questions, not to tell a story.

Creativity

Unlike hard-news reporting, in soft news you have ample opportunities to be creative. You get to flex your imagination muscles.

Feature writers often employ unusual angles. For example, a writer might report on the destruction of an old brick school building from the perspective of one of the bricks.

Feature writers also use sensory imagery. The phrase "show, don't tell" could be considered a rule for feature writers. Don't *tell* readers an athlete is exhausted. Instead, *show* them by describing the athlete's labored breathing and sweat-soaked skin.

Because you have a longer leash when you write features, you have to be extra careful that you don't stray too far. Remember the qualities of journalistic writing: The reporting is accurate and objective, and the writing is clear, concise, and colorful.

Types of Features

Journalists disagree about whether all features entertain *and* inform. Most agree that features can be categorized into these general types, each with a special purpose:

News feature: a story that offers a human-interest view on a hard news event

Informative feature: a story that presents practical information on an interesting subject

Personality profile: a story that reveals the personality of someone through incidents, anecdotes, and quotes (not through a list of accomplishments, favorite things, or biographical facts)

Human-interest feature: a short piece (about 100 words), told in a unique or clever way, that concentrates on an unusual and emotionally appealing subject (person, place, object, or animal)

Historical feature: a story about an interesting aspect of a historical subject, gathered from research and interviews

Personal-accomplishment feature: a story that focuses on an individual who accomplished something amazing or who has overcome a particular life struggle

Shared-experience feature: a story that shares information gained from the writer's firsthand experience in doing something

How-to feature: a story that explains how to do something

Featurizing Hard News

Electronic media can give the public hard-news reports around the clock. To compete, newspapers have to do something different. More and more, they give hard news a soft-news angle. They **featurize** it. These featurized news stories may or may not utilize in-depth reporting (p. 81).

School newspapers commonly featurize news. A tornado that hits your town is hard news. Your school paper can't report it when it happens, but you can featurize it in a dozen different ways. Here are a few to illustrate the idea:

- Do an informative feature. Explain how tornadoes form. Add a quick-read menu checklist for tornado safety.
- Do an in-depth news feature. Show how people survived when their homes were struck. Include a sidebar on Tornado Alley, the area of the country most commonly hit by tornadoes. Add a quick-read menu list of the 10 deadliest tornadoes ever to strike your state.
- Do a human-interest feature. Trace the emotional experience of a child or an animal during the tornado.
- Do a historical feature. Cover natural disasters in your area, including tornadoes. Include period photographs.

Press Time

Walter Cronkite, a legend in print and broadcast journalism, discovered his calling as editor of his high school paper, *Campus Cub.* During his career, Cronkite covered events ranging from the Nazi trials at Nuremberg to the 1969 moon landing. Cronkite is critical of today's tendency to featurize everything and "doll up the news." He says that featurizing may distort rather than improve reporting. He also says that a focus on features takes time away from reporting more substantial news.

Writing Absorbing Features

One of the best ways to learn feature writing is by example. Take time to read features. Note what works and what doesn't work.

Take time also to review the guidelines for clear, concise, and colorful writing (p. 40), writing captivating leads (p. 48), and using quotes correctly (pp. 52–56). In addition, here are some other tips.

TIPS Writing Absorbing Features

- Choose an interesting, unusual subject. For example, instead of writing a feature on fashion trends, write a feature on fashion that has endured over time, such as blue jeans.
- Remember: show, don't tell. Present details that let the reader see, smell, hear, taste, and touch the elements in the story.
- Personalize and localize your features. Whatever the topic, try to involve real people from your school and community. (And don't just focus on the "in" crowd.)
- Keep an open mind. Don't begin a feature assignment with preconceived ideas.
- Draw information from several primary sources and a good sampling of secondary sources (pp. 19–20).
- Don't spend too much time setting the scene. Get to the people and events of the story quickly.
- Use the devices of fiction writers. Read, read, read, to see how writers describe characters, build suspense, and establish a mood.
- Use only one anecdote, example, or quote to get across an idea.
- Build to a strong ending that reemphasizes your angle.

Sports

Action is the byword for sports coverage: REPORT action. CELEBRATE action. PROMOTE action.

Sportswriting is one of the most action-packed fields of journalism. The best sports pages are full of lively writing and exciting photographs.

Sports are more varied than ever, and school sportswriters get to cover a wide range of action. Increasingly, this includes not only competitive, school-sponsored sports but also recreational sports.

Timely coverage of sports is tough for school newspapers. Other media have already reported the outcomes of most sports events. That means, as a sportswriter for your school paper, you'll probably be writing sports features, which may or may not be tied to a sports event. You'll also write advance and coverage stories, but even these are usually featurized. This is your chance to tell the story the other papers missed!

Covering Sports Events

As a sportswriter, attend as many sports events as possible. Follow the event as if you were doing hard-news reporting, but don't hesitate to get the details for soft-news coverage too.

Here's what you need to do:

- Position yourself where you can clearly see the action but where you're not in the way of athletes or coaches. Don't sit in the stands. You can easily miss action if your view is blocked.
- Take detailed, accurate notes of nearly everything that happens. (Learn to watch the action and take legible notes at the same time.) In your notes, underline spectacular moves or turning points in the action so you can play these up in your stories.
- Remember that you're a reporter, not a cheerleader. Don't let your partisanship affect your objectivity. Take notes on significant action by your athletes, their opponents, and the crowd.
- Observe and take notes on how weather or the condition of the playing area affects the action.
- Get to the event before the athletes and stay after everyone is gone. Hit the locker rooms if you're allowed admittance. Talk to athletes, coaches, fans, cheerleaders, officials, and anyone else who may have facts or opinions that can add to your story.

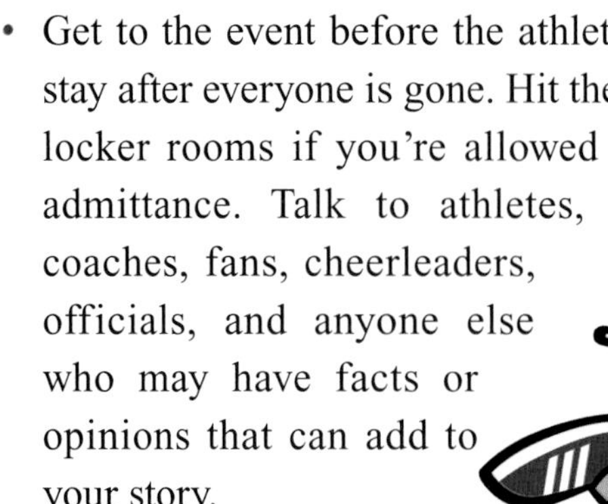

Pregame Stories

An advance story is called a **pregame story** in sports journalism. Pregame stories include the 5 W's and H early in the story. The *when* and *where* of the event should be announced no later than the nut graph (p. 45).

Pregame stories quote sources from your school and the opponent school. For that reason, you need to have connections with coaches, athletes, and sportswriters at other schools.

Pregame stories typically include a rundown of the following:

- the previous year's score
- condition of athletes
- key athletes or starting lineups
- comparisons of team or individual records
- comments on styles of play
- significance of the event in terms of records or future events
- any history of rivalries

Featurizing Pregame Stories

Pregame stories are generally featurized and have a unique angle (p. 25). Consider one of the following to featurize your story:

- Highlight an activity leading up to the event, such as plans for a special pep assembly or details on a special training session.
- Focus on background such as a historical rivalry or a tradition surrounding the event.
- Stress the significance of the event in terms of its potential impact on an individual's achievement.
- Present the various superstitions and rituals athletes engage in before a big sports event.

Postgame Stories

A **postgame story** in sports is essentially a coverage story. It should never be a play-by-play rehash of the event.

In general, sports coverage should concentrate on future rather than past events. A postgame story does, however, give a reporter the chance to do the following:

- update records of individuals and teams
- explain confusing or controversial rulings
- offer insight into event highlights and low points
- analyze the *hows* and *whys* of the event

Featurizing Postgame Stories

Postgame stories are nearly always featurized. At their best, they emphasize the drama of the sports event. To do this, you have to find an angle that recaptures the atmosphere of the event and the emotion of critical moments. These are some possibilities:

- Offer a side-by-side comparison of the event, using viewpoints of athletes from your school and from the opposing school.
- Focus on one grand or grueling moment of the event, and let the athletes involved explain their thoughts and feelings at the time.
- Cover the interaction among fans, cheerleaders, athletes, and coaches during the event.

Sports Features

Sports features are just like any other features except that they're about sports and recreation topics. They may or may not have a news peg (p. 87).

Running Features

Vary the types of features you offer (p. 90). You might, however, have one or two **running features.** A running feature is a feature of one type that appears, or runs, in each issue.

Personality profiles, shared-experience features, informative features, and how-to features are common choices for running features. For example, you might do a running informative feature on sports technology.

Single-Focus Features

Another popular approach for sports features is to focus on one sport or form of recreation in each issue. Focus on something that's in season. That is, don't profile snow skiing in the summer.

For your single-focus features, run two or more types of features with different angles on the topic. Make at least one of the features an information feature or a how-to feature so readers get solid information on background, equipment, and techniques. Add sidebars.

Press Time

The team locker room is a common place for sportswriters to conduct postgame interviews. But in 1977, the New York Yankees baseball team banned *Sports Illustrated* reporter Melissa Ludtke from their locker room because of her sex. Ludtke sued the Yankees and won the case. Since then female reporters have been granted the same access privileges as male reporters. Ludtke covered track star Carl Lewis at the 1983 Olympics for *Time* magazine. No reporters are allowed locker-room interviews at the Olympics.

Sports Shorts

Many schools aim for broad, balanced sports coverage. At the same time, they want to devote more space to sports features.

One way to achieve this goal is to condense events coverage. You can, for example, combine pregame and postgame stories. Another option is to cover sports events with sports "shorts" that capture relevant information and provide a record of events.

Sports shorts can be set up like news briefs (p. 77) or in an outline format. List home scores first.

Sports Shorts

Freshman Girls Soccer

Scores: Northfield 4, La Grange 2; Northfield 3, Dayton 2; Northfield 0, Brighton 5

Highlights: Jill Vega, 8th grade, scored a last-minute goal on a pass from Claire Sloan, 8th grade, to secure the Dayton win. Muddy fields played a part in the Lions defeat at Brighton.

Coming up: at Fayette April 4; hosting Lyle April 8

Scoreboard

Sports shorts may be accompanied by a "scoreboard." The scoreboard consists of charts showing current records for various sports. Note that all records are current as of "press time." This means that you updated scores just before the pages went to be printed or photocopied.

Sportswriters

Sportswriters are a special breed. To be a good sportswriter, you must enjoy sports. But it takes more than that. Here are a few of the basic requirements for a sportswriter:

- Know the rules, strategies, schedules, and statistics of each sport you cover.
- Understand the style of play of your school's athletes and those of opposing schools in the sports event.
- Develop skill at detecting strengths and weaknesses in individual athletes and teams.
- Be able to follow, and take accurate notes on, fast-moving action.
- Be able to recognize key moments in a sports event and to analyze the overall significance of the event.
- Be able to interpret and present the emotions and action of the event to readers.
- Develop a productive, ongoing relationship with coaches and athletes.
- Commit to attending practices as well as sports events to get a firsthand perspective on a story.
- Deliver accurate, fair, and complete coverage.

Writing Winning Sports Stories

The key to writing winning sports stories is to be informed and informal, organized and original. Aside from that, here are a few specific tips.

TIPS Writing Winning Sports Stories

- Do your research! Go into an interview prepared with background on the sport, issues, and records.
- Schedule regular interviews with coaches and athletes—preseason, midseason, and postseason. It'll add perspective to your stories.
- Ask questions that will generate out-of-the-ordinary quotes. Try to get anecdotes (p. 89) and colorful descriptions of specific moments from your sources.
- Make sure any stats you use are meaningful to the readers. Double-check them with the statistician or manager.
- Find an angle that will make readers sit up and take notice.
- Avoid being cutesy or complex for the sake of originality.
- Avoid clichés (p. 41). If you've heard it, it's clichéd.
- Avoid jargon (p. 41) unless it's part of a particularly colorful quote. If it may confuse any readers, explain it.
- Keep a list of strong verbs handy to enliven your stories.
- Don't overdo imagery, especially in the lead. Keep it punchy.
- Read sports in the professional and school press regularly.
- Maintain a sports clippings file (articles from other papers about your teams and opponents) for background information.

Objectivity in Sportswriting

Readers expect sportswriters to make judgments. It's traditional. But if all you do is rant about rival teams and rave about star players, you're not doing your job. You may be a sports fan, but you're a reporter first.

Follow these guidelines to maintain an appropriate level of objectivity in sportswriting:

- Be enthusiastic about your home team, but maintain a fair, unbiased perspective about opponents.
- When you analyze or predict outcomes of sports events, support each opinion with factual examples that prove your point.
- Balance events coverage by quoting a wide variety of athletes, fans, managers, cheerleaders, and coaches.
- Don't glorify star athletes. Support teamwork.
- Balance overall sports and recreation coverage. Include coverage of students who engage in noncompetitive sports and recreation for fun.

Press Time

One of the earliest sportswriters was William Barclay "Bat" Masterson. Before moving to New York City in 1902 to become a journalist, Masterson had been a famous gambler and gunslinger throughout the Wild West, as well as a scout, a buffalo hunter, and a deputy marshall of Dodge City, Kansas (where he worked with his friend, the legendary Wyatt Earp). A TV show based on Bat Masterson's western adventures aired in the late 1950s and early 1960s.

Editorials

"Opinions cannot survive if no one has a chance to fight for them."

—*Thomas Mann, author*

An **editorial** is a short article that expresses opinions on a topic. By strict definition, an editorial expresses the official opinion of the newspaper. As such, an editorial doesn't have a **byline.** A byline tells who wrote a story.

The editorial board (p. 10) decides which topics to tackle and what to say about them. Topics may range from truancy laws to sexism.

Any reporter or editor may be assigned to write an editorial. Editorial writers sometimes use the pronoun *we,* or the "editorial *we,*" to state opinions. Or you can use the paper's name.

Newspapers allow an individual to express personal opinions on a topic in various types of opinion articles. These articles are always bylined. They often use the first-person pronoun *I.* Readers can assume that the opinions expressed are those of the writer only.

Writing Editorials

In general, these are the steps in the process of writing an editorial:

1. The editorial board reviews possible topics for editorials at its regular meeting to plan the next issue.
2. The editorial board members discuss the topics in detail. They vote on the topics to cover and commit to a stand on each.
3. The board assigns a reporter or editor to write each editorial.
4. The writer researches the topic, consulting a variety of sources. If the facts appear to conflict with the opinions of the editorial board, the writer informs members. The board may change its position.
5. The writer completes the editorial.
6. The editorial board reviews the editorial. The members suggest changes, if necessary. Then they approve it.

Structure for Editorials

Most editorials (and other opinion articles) have a similar structure. Use this general structure as your guide:

Introduction: State your opinion on the topic. Give brief background if necessary.

Body: Explain your position. Provide support with facts, examples, and expert opinions on the topic. Include any opposing opinions first and follow with yours.

Conclusion: Comment on solutions or restate your position.

Many editorial writers use the traditional five-paragraph essay structure. The first paragraph is your introduction. The second paragraph explains your position. The third presents opposing opinions. The fourth presents your opinions, which refute the opposing opinons. The final paragraph is your conclusion.

Topics for Editorials

You can find topics for editorials the same way you find news and feature stories. Listen to the buzz. What are people talking about? concerned about?

Many editorials have a news peg (p. 87). Most newspapers include at least one editorial on an important topic covered elsewhere in the paper.

Use these questions to test whether the topic is a good candidate for an editorial:

- Does this topic possess elements of news (p. 17), or pass the "Who cares?" test (p. 17)?
- Can this topic be localized (p. 25) so that readers see its relevance to their own lives?
- Is there a strong need to tell readers something on this topic that can't be presented in a news or feature story?
- Do you have time to research this topic thoroughly so that you can present an informed opinion?
- Are you prepared to take full responsibility for the facts and opinions expressed in an editorial on this topic?

Functions of Editorials

What do you want your editorial to do? What is its function?

Editorials are often defined by functions such as those that follow. You may want your editorial to serve more than one function. It may persuade and entertain. It may praise and explain. It may persuade and entertain and explain. Okay, but try to determine its primary function and let that one be your guiding force.

Editorials That Persuade

Editorials that persuade are intended to convince readers to follow a particular way of thinking on an issue. To present a persuasive case, you must carefully cover both sides of the issue.

These editorials usually concentrate on something that needs to change. Sometimes they simply point out the perceived problem. More often, they include a call to action.

For editorials that persuade, use this organization:

1. Define the problem as you see it.
2. Present the opinions of the other side.
3. Refute each point made by the opposing side with your opinions. Support each opinion with facts.
4. Offer one or more logical solutions to the problem.
5. Ask someone to do something specific to solve the problem.

Press Time

Horace Greeley, founder of the *New York Tribune*, is considered the father of the editorial page. His *Tribune* editorials against slavery, liquor, and corruption reached a huge audience. In 1862, during the height of the Civil War, his anti-slavery editorial, "Prayer of Twenty Millions" reached President Abraham Lincoln. Lincoln wrote a personal response to Greeley stressing his primary aim to "save the Union." A draft of the Emancipation Proclamation lay in Lincoln's desk drawer when Greeley's editorial was published. Soon after, Lincoln signed it.

Editorials That Explain

Editorials that explain are intended to interpret for readers the meaning or significance of an event or situation. Your job is to inform, not persuade.

Topics for these editorials often rise out of complicated conditions created by a gradual or a sudden change that affects readers. For example, the editorial might suggest or hypothesize why the student council is sponsoring fewer events than in past years. Or it might offer reasons why a teacher suddenly quit in the middle of the year.

Follow this organization for editorials that explain:

1. Tell what happened or state the situation.
2. Explain in detail what caused the event to happen or the situation to occur. The explanation may include background information and examination of motives.
3. Interpret the importance of the event or situation. This interpretation may include listing possible consequences.

Editorials That Praise

Editorials that praise are intended to honor, commend, or congratulate an individual, an organization, an institution, or a group. The editorial should outline the reason for the praise, including significant events leading up to it.

For example, if you were writing an editorial to congratulate the Odyssey of the Mind team on winning the state championship, you would cite the accomplishments of the team. You would also mention the difficulties involved in training and competition.

An editorial that praises might be organized as follows:

1. Announce who or what is to be praised.
2. Cite reasons for the praise, providing specific examples to support your reasons. This may include comparing the subject to others not as worthy of praise.
3. Ask readers to share in praising the subject. This type of conclusion is optional.

Editorials That Entertain

Editorials that entertain are intended to poke fun at a topic. Topics treated with this type of editorial don't need heavy criticism or a serious tone. For example, you might want to comment on music that your parents listen to, or where and when fellow students use cell phones.

Keep it lighthearted. Try satire. With satire, you use humor and wit to slyly suggest a need for improvement.

Satire can be biting or gentle. But stay away from sarcasm. Sarcasm is a mean-spirited form of satire in which you pretend to praise but actually condemn. You should come across as funny, not nasty.

Be creative about the way you organize an editorial that entertains. Think of it as a short feature that expresses opinions.

Make your angle and organization suit your topic. For the topic of cell phones, for example, you might set up the editorial as a telephone conversation. For the topic of music across the generations, you might pretend to be writing in the future about the way your grandchildren view music from your generation.

Writing Effective Editorials

Editorials have the potential to influence readers in profound ways. Take your responsibility *seriously.* But try to enjoy experimenting with ways to write effective editorials. Here are some tips to help you out.

TIPS Writing Effective Editorials

- Choose topics that are interesting and relevant to the majority of your readers. Editorials on obscure topics have limited impact.
- Write about a current issue. Don't harp on something that has been decided months ago.
- Don't shy away from controversial topics. Tackle them if they're important for your readers.
- Don't begin with a question. You'll prompt readers to start thinking about their own views, not yours.
- Make your point clearly and get to it quickly. If readers are confused or bored, you're sunk. Keep it under 300 words.
- Be sincere. If you have a strong conviction in your opinion, readers will sense it.
- Research your topic thoroughly.
- Be fair. Present facts and opinions from both sides.
- Support all opinions with facts.
- Keep personalities out of it. Personal attacks are inappropriate.
- Make sure your solutions are logical and practical.
- Make your conclusion leave readers with a clear understanding of your opinion. Stimulate readers to think and feel.

The Editorial Page

The **editorial page** is the page in your newspaper that's devoted to opinions. The page facing the editorial page is called the **op-ed page,** or opposite-editorial page. Editorials are placed on the editorial page. Other opinion articles may appear on the op-ed page.

Editorial Policy

Your newspaper should print and stand by an **editorial policy.** The editorial policy explains the goals and policy of the newspaper. This policy is often printed on your editorial page. It may be an abbreviated version of a longer policy.

The editorial policy may include any or all of the following:

- goals of the newspaper
- information about funding and distribution, including the number of issues printed per year
- policies regarding content (who writes it and governs it), advertising, and corrections of printed errors
- ethical and legal guidelines followed
- guidelines for letters to the editor (p. 110)

Masthead

Also appearing on the editorial page is the **masthead.** The masthead is usually boxed in a lower corner. It's printed in smaller type than the stories and should not draw attention to itself.

Although it's played down, the masthead states important publication information, including the following:

- the name of the paper
- the **volume number,** which refers to the number of years the paper has been in existence

- the **issue number,** which refers to the consecutive number of issues for the year
- the names of the editorial board members and sometimes other staff members
- the name of the adviser
- contact information such as address and phone number
- the editorial policy
- the cost, if any, and other distribution information

Letters to the Editor

A **letter to the editor** is a short letter from a reader expressing an opinion. A reader may respond to an editorial your paper has printed or may write about another issue of concern. Letters to the editor are often printed on the same page as staff editorials.

Encourage letters to the editor. Print a request on your editorial page that asks for signed and sincere opinions. You might leave a box in the administrative office so that those who wish to submit letters may do so conveniently. Be prepared to print both critical and complimentary letters.

Before printing any letters to the editor, however, verify that the letter did indeed come from the person who signed it. Keep all original letters on file until the next issue just in case you need one of them to solve a legal problem.

Give each letter a brief headline identifying the topic. Add one larger headline identifying the copy as letters to the editor.

Make readers aware of guidelines for letters. Your editorial policy should state the following about letters to the editor:

- whether or not letters to the editor may be published unsigned
- maximum length (usually 250 words)
- your right to edit for clarity, to refuse any letter for any reason, and to limit the number of letters from one person in a given period

Point-Counterpoint Articles

Readers are attracted to opposing views presented side by side, especially if the topic is controversial. Two (or more) opinion articles from people on opposite sides of an issue, printed side by side, are known as **point-counterpoint** articles.

The writers may or may not be members of the newspaper staff. Make sure these guest writers can write. Get their agreement that their copy may be edited as necessary.

Point-counterpoint articles are often run on the op-ed page. They must be bylined. Include a lead-in explaining who the writers are and why they were chosen to represent the two views.

Random Opinion Polls

One of the most popular type of opinion articles is the **random opinion poll.** It poses a question on an editorial topic to a small group of people (four or five). Each person's opinion is printed, often next to his or her photo.

Represent a range of opinions in your poll. That means you need to ask more than a few people—and take more than a few photos. Choose those that are most interesting.

Strive for equal representation of respondents. You should have a balance of male and female, and represent all grades.

Editorial Cartoons

An **editorial cartoon** uses a picture instead of words to get a point across. It may illustrate an editorial or stand alone. Because it's an editorial, it expresses the opinion of the newspaper. But unlike editorials, it's signed. Most editorial cartoons are printed on the editorial page.

Whereas many people won't read an entire written editorial, nearly all readers will read an editorial cartoon. If you want to share your views in a creative way, this is an art form worth developing.

Skills for Editorial Cartooning

To be a good editorial cartoonist, develop the following skills:

- artistic skill, especially in drawing
- visual communication skills—in particular, the ability to communicate an opinion clearly by combining a picture with words
- skill at identifying newsworthy events and attitudes—in school and in the world at large
- skill at using humor to make a point

Press Time

Thomas Nast was among the earliest American editorial cartoonists, and he remains one of history's most influential ones. He created scathing cartoons during the 1870s about the corrupt political boss of New York City politics, William M. Tweed. These cartoons resulted in Tweed's fall from power. Tweed fled to Spain, where he was arrested by Spanish officials. They recognized him from Nast's caricatures in *Harper's Weekly*, a widely circulated American magazine.

TIPS Drawing Editorial Cartoons

- Study editorial cartoons. Your library may have books on editorial cartooning, and most city dailies publish cartoons each day.
- Begin simply. Use strong, clean lines. Keep background to a minimum unless it's essential to the meaning.
- Make the most important visual features stand out. Use contrast to emphasize a part of the cartoon.
- Keep proportions somewhat normal. Exaggerate for a reason.
- Avoid using too many words. Make them large and legible.
- Stress meaning. You will eventually develop a personal style; but if it clouds the meaning, the cartoon fails.
- Begin with pencil sketches. Test them on people to see how they work. Revise until the meaning is clear. Then polish the drawing, using a dark pen or pencil for the final draft.

Columns

An editorial reflects a consensus of the editorial board. A **column** is an opinion article that reflects the opinion of an individual writer. It carries a byline.

The opinion of a columnist isn't necessarily the opinion of the newspaper. School-newspaper columnists may represent a wide range of viewpoints on a wide range of topics.

Columns usually appear on the editorial page. They can, however, pop up elsewhere, depending on the topic. If you're writing on a sports topic, for example, you might run your column on the sports page. Just make sure it's clearly identified as an opinion article.

Columns may be running features (p. 00), written by the same person in each issue. If they're well-written and show individuality and originality, they'll draw a following. Faithful fans will read their favorite columnist before they read anything else. These running columns usually have a name that relays the spirit and style of the writer. Many carry a photo of the writer to add human interest.

TIPS Writing Columns

- Be yourself. If you want to develop a personal style, it's the only place to start.
- Remember that you're talking to readers, not writing in a personal journal. Imagine talking to them from your kitchen table or someplace you feel relaxed and sociable.
- Look for odd, unusual angles on a topic.
- Keep your columns short (450–750 words).
- Go ahead and "bury the lead." That is, don't state your opinion right up front. Make readers curious about where you stand on an issue until they're well into the column.

- Include other viewpoints to add perspective.
- Use examples and anecdotes to illustrate your points.
- Credit sources that helped you form your opinions.
- Vary your tone from column to column. If you're always angry or sympathetic, readers will find your columns predictable.
- Stretch your wings. Try something new. But make sure whatever you try is "in synch" with your angle and tone.
- Be careful not to concentrate too often on your own family and experiences. Don't become a legend in your own mind.
- Steer clear of advice columns and gossip columns. Student journalists can get into difficult legal situations by giving advice on sensitive issues. And passing along the rumors that constitute most gossip is even more risky.

Press Time

Ambrose Bierce was a writer noted for his biting satire. In 1877 he began writing his immensely popular column "Prattle" for San Francisco's *Argonaut*. Ten years later he moved his column to a larger publication, the *San Francisco Examiner*, and his fame spread throughout the West. At age 72 Bierce traveled to Mexico to write about the Mexican Revolution. He never returned. The last word from Bierce was a letter he sent from Chihuahua in December of 1913.

Reviews

A **review** is another opportunity for you to express your opinion without the official approval of the editorial board. In a review, you share your personal opinion on the worth of a product or performance with your readers.

Most reviews in school papers revolve around entertainment and so appear in the entertainment section. Common items reviewed include movies, books, plays, restaurants, video games, web sites, live concerts, and CDs.

Your review may do one or more of the following:

- Itemize the strengths and weaknesses of a product or performance.
- Compare and contrast one product or performance with another of the same type.
- Evaluate a product or performance on the basis of how well it fulfills its intended purpose.

Press Time

Gene Siskel and Roger Ebert formed one of the most celebrated partnerships in journalism history. Siskel, who died in 1999, was a film critic for the *Chicago Tribune*. Ebert wrote for the *Chicago Sun-Times*. Together they reviewed movies on a syndicated TV show that began in 1975. The name of the show, *Siskel & Ebert*, was determined early in the partnership when Siskel won a coin flip to see whose name would come first. The trademark "thumbs up/thumbs down" judgment on movies they reviewed was Ebert's invention.

Ratings Devices

Reviews should do more than offer a thumbs up/thumbs down rating. Ratings devices such as stars or thumbs up/thumbs down signals merely label an item as good, mediocre, or bad. Of course, you can use ratings devices. They do serve a function. But accompany ratings with reviews that truly analyze the merits of the product or performance.

TIPS Writing Reviews

- Keep in mind that your review should serve your readers. Don't write solely for yourself.
- Concentrate on meaningful characteristics, not petty points, of the product or performance.
- Support your opinions with specific examples.
- Read various kinds of reviews to understand better the criteria used to evaluate different kinds of products and performances.
- Watch performances more than once and use products many times before you formulate solid views. Get other perspectives too. Talk to other viewers and users.
- Don't just parrot other reviewers. Make your own judgments.
- Make your reviews timely. Don't review a movie if it'll be gone when your paper is printed.
- When you review student products or performances, don't hold them to the same standards as professional ones. Look for good points to go along with any bad points.

1 **Explore Your World** In a local newspaper, read one news, feature, and sports story, and one editorial. Is the news story an advance or a coverage story? Is it featurized? Was it reported in-depth? If so, was it significant and stimulating? If you read a survey story, how were the results presented? Perhaps you read a consumer report. If so, what approach was used?

Does the feature exhibit all the characteristics of feature stories? What type of feature is it? Does it have a local angle?

Was the sports story a pregame story, a postgame story, or a sport feature? Was the writing informed, informal, organized, and original? Was it action-oriented? objective?

How about the editorial? Does the topic seem a good candidate for an editorial? What was the function of the editorial? Do you think it fulfilled its function well? Why?

2 **Expand Your Skills** Choose one type of story you think you'd like to write for your school paper—news, feature, sports, or editorial. Select a topic. Make a list of everything you must do to write a good story of that type on that topic. Draw upon the information in this chapter and Chapter 3, especially the tips. Are you ready to do it? Talk to your editor and take a shot.

3 **Express Yourself** In your Journalist's Notebook, write a column. Let it express not only your opinions on a topic, but your personality as well. You might want to read a few columns in your school paper or the daily press for inspiration. Give your column a title suitable for a running feature. Add a headline.

Copyediting and Proofreading

HMMMM
DICTIONARY
FINAL PROOF

Copyediting

You've written your masterpiece. It's perfect. You hand it over for editing. You get it back. It's covered with red ink. Okay, so it's not perfect . . . yet.

Whenever you make changes to improve your copy, you're **editing.** The editing process involves cooperation among reporters, section editors, and copy editors. It takes teamwork and time. Teamwork and time will make your copy perfect.

The process of editing copy occurs in several phases. The final phase of editing before it's dropped into pages is called **copyediting.**

You may edit or copyedit copy electronically on the computer screen. Or you may prefer to print out **hard copy,** text on paper, and edit manually on the printout first. (That's where the red ink comes in.) Whether you work electronically or manually, you'll perform the same basic tasks in each phase of the process.

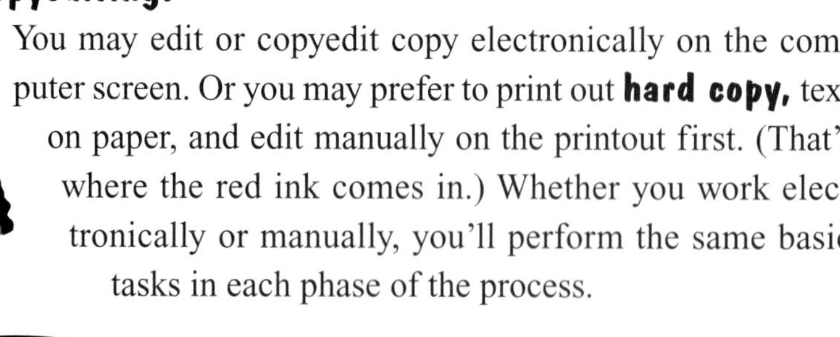

The Editing Process

This is a rough overview of steps in the editing process:

1. The reporter writes and edits the first draft.
2. The section editor edits it further, as necessary. The reporter and section editor may work together on this step.
3. The copy editor (or another editor) does the copyediting.
4. The section editor approves the final copy.
5. The section editor turns over final copy to the design staff. If you don't have a copy editor, this is done after step 2.

Copyfitting

What if the edited copy doesn't quite fit in its spot on the pages? You *make* it fit. This part of the process is called **copyfitting.**

Copyfitting may require adding information. If the story turns out to be very short, you might add a sidebar (p. 62). You might also add a boxed trivia question related to copy on the page or art to illustrate something in the copy.

You may opt to **jump,** or continue, the story to another page; however, there's no guarantee space will be available on other pages. Never jump a story to one page and then jump it again to another location.

Usually copyfitting requires you to cut. Stories written in the inverted-pyramid format are easy to cut. Other stories must be trimmed by careful editing. Just make sure you don't alter the sense of a sentence or disrupt the logical flow of ideas.

Journalistic Style

At every stage of the editing process, you need to apply your newspaper's **style.** This isn't style in the sense of a writer's special way of writing. In this sense, style is the way copy should be written to be consistent within a publication.

The rules and guidelines for your newspaper's style should be included in an easy-to-follow **stylebook.** Your newspaper's stylebook specifies the standards for such things as abbreviations, punctuation, and italicizing. Everyone on staff must follow the stylebook to ensure that all copy adheres to these standards throughout each issue.

Many of the style standards your newspaper uses will be the same as those used by papers all over the country. Others will be applicable just to your newspaper.

Several organizations publish journalistic stylebooks. Most professional journalists use the Associated Press or the *New York Times* style. Quill and Scroll Society and the Columbia Scholastic Press Association publish stylebooks for student journalists. You probably use one of these or one customized for your paper. If you don't have a stylebook, consider using the one that begins on page 245.

Copy Editors

You may copyedit your own stories or have a dedicated copy editor on staff. It takes time and training to be a good copy editor. These are the requirements you should strive to meet:

- Know your newspaper stylebook inside and out.
- Be an exceptional speller and have a strong working knowledge of grammar, punctuation, and word usage.
- Challenge and check the accuracy of information in the copy.

- Have a broad knowledge of your school, local community, and the global community.
- Know the policies and procedures of your school paper.
- Be a reliable judge of effective, well-written copy.
- Be a skilled writer, able to improve poorly written copy.
- Be able to recognize editorializing and edit it out as necessary.
- Be able to see details as well as the overall scope of the copy.
- Refrain from blindly applying rules that don't improve the copy.
- Develop a constructive relationship with reporters and editors.

If you print a factual error, you should print a **retraction.** A retraction is an admission of a mistake. It should appear in the next issue in the same section where the mistake occurred under the heading "Correction." A retraction should state what was printed and when (what issue), as well as the correct information.

Press Time

Several New York newspaper publishers formed the Harbor News Association in 1848. The association sent out a single steamboat to meet ships arriving from Europe and retrieve any news they brought. In addition, the association used the telegraph to retrieve news from across the nation. Newspapers could buy news from the association for much less than the cost of retrieving it themselves. The Harbor News Association grew into one of the most respected journalism organizations in the world: the Associated Press.

Copyediting Tasks

Here's one way to organize your copyediting tasks:

1. Read the copy to see if it includes all important information. Ask the reporter to supply what's missing or get it yourself.
2. Delete any improper or irrelevant information.
3. Verify questionable facts. Use more than one source.
4. Check attribution for every opinion and any controversial fact (p. 51). Add attributions if necessary.
5. Edit out any editorializing, unless the copy is an editorial, column, or review. Confirm that all opinions in editorials and other opinion articles are supported by facts.
6. Check the effectiveness of the lead. It should include essential information and introduce the angle. It should also be brief, captivating, and appropriate in tone.
7. Check the organization of the story to see that it makes sense. Rearrange paragraphs if necessary.
8. Edit to improve the writing. Check paragraphing and transitions. Ideas should flow smoothly and logically. Simplify and tighten up by following the tips on page 41.
9. Verify the spellings of all names, places, and organizations.
10. Verify and add missing identification: titles and grades.
11. Verify all dates and times.
12. Correct all errors in style and mechanics (grammar, punctuation, word usage, and spelling).
13. Reread and fix anything missed.

Copyediting Tools and Resources

These are the tools and resources you need for copyediting tasks:

Stylebook: Keep it on hand. Use it. Know it. Abide by it.

Spell checker: This is available on all word processors. Customize it to include frequently used names, such as the name of your school and city. Note that a spell checker won't question a word that's spelled correctly—even if you used it incorrectly. *Too, to, two*—do you know the difference? You probably do, but your spell checker doesn't. Check your story first for wrong usage.

Dictionaries: Equip your newsroom with several up-do-date dictionaries. Use a dictionary to check a word's meaning, spelling, endings for tenses, plural forms, and hyphenation.

Thesaurus: Use a thesaurus when you need to find alternatives for a word—or exactly the right word. Most word-processing programs have a thesaurus but a print one is handy.

Grammar handbook: Make it a simple one for quick reference.

Telephone book: Keep a local phone book handy to verify spellings of names, phone numbers, and addresses.

School directory or homeroom list: Refer to official school documents such as these to verify spellings of student, faculty, and staff names, as well as grades and titles.

Almanac: Clear up questions about well-known people, places, and events with an almanac for the current year.

CD-ROM encyclopedia: Use this resource to check facts quickly. It's indispensable when the library isn't open.

Copyediting Symbols

To make copyediting on hard copy easier, neater, and more efficient, editors use a set of standard copyediting symbols.

Explanation	Mark in Margin	Mark in Copy	Corrected Copy
delete letter		the careful rreader	the careful reader
delete word		the careful reader	the reader
close up space		the careful r eader	the careful reader
delete and close up		the careful reeader	the careful reader
insert letter		the creful reader	the careful reader
insert word		the reader	the careful reader
change word		the cautious reader	the careful reader
lowercase letter	lc	The careful reader	the careful reader
lowercase letters	lc x 3	The Careful Reader	the careful reader
lowercase word	lc	THE careful reader	the careful reader
italicize	ital	the careful reader	the *careful* reader
roman type	rom	the *careful* reader	the careful reader
boldface type	bf	the careful reader	the **careful** reader
small capital letters	sc	The Careful Reader	THE CAREFUL READER
capital letter	cap	the careful reader	The careful reader
capital words	cap	the careful reader	THE CAREFUL READER
transpose letters	tr	the craeful reader	the careful reader
transpose words	tr	the reader careful	the careful reader
ignore correction	stet	the careful reader	the careful reader

Explanation	Mark in Margin	Mark in Copy	Corrected Copy
spell out	(sp)	(2) careful readers	two careful readers
begin paragraph	¶	Do you know any careful readers? We need one.	Do you know any careful readers? We need one.
no paragraph; run in	(run in)	Do you know any careful readers? We need one.	Do you know any careful readers? We need one.
query	(careful?) or (?) or (OK?)	Are you a reader?	Are you a careful reader?
insert space		thecareful reader	the careful reader
insert period		The careful reader	The careful reader.
insert comma		the careful attentive reader	the careful, attentive reader
insert colon		the careful reader	the careful reader:
insert apostrophe		the careful readers guide	the careful reader's guide
insert quotation marks		the careful reader	"the careful reader"
parentheses		the careful reader	the (careful) reader
hyphen		Read word for word	Read word-for-word
align	(align)	the careful reader	the careful reader
begin new line		Reading carefully is something not every person can do.	Reading carefully is something not every person can do.
bad break	(bb) or ev·er·y·one	Reading carefully is not something ever- yone can do.	Reading carefully is not something every- one can do.
wrong font	(wf)	the careful reader	the careful reader
widow or orphan	(widow)	The careful read- er.	The careful reader

Formatting Copy

Most reporters write copy directly on the computer. All copy should be formatted the same by all reporters. This makes it easier for copyeditors. It also makes it possible to estimate how much copy will fit on a page. Depending on the width of your columns and the type used, for example, you might estimate that 25 lines of copy equals 6 column inches.

Follow these guidelines when you format copy to hand over to an editor:

- Use common, readable type for all copy.
- Double-space your copy and give it wide margins on each side.
- Type the file name in the upper left-hand corner. Your file name should include the writer's initials, the year, the issue number, and the **slug,** a word or phrase that identifies the copy.
- Under the file name, type the date.
- Under the date, type the byline.
- Skip two lines and begin the copy.
- Type the file name, date, and page number in angle brackets (<LA995winter blues page 3>), at the top of each page. Or include this information in the header. The header will automatically print on every page but isn't visible on the screen.
- Indicate the end of the story. Try a traditional journalism indicator: -end-, 30, or ###. Center this on a separate line.
- Back up your file. Store one copy on your hard drive and one on a disk. Print out a hard copy too. At the end of each page of hard copy, if the story goes on, write "more" and circle it.
- Make a copy of the story available to your editor. You might send the file to your editor's computer as an e-mail attachment or put it on a disk and hand it over. If copyediting is done on paper instead of electronically, provide a hard copy to the editor.

Proofreading

Proofreading is often confused with copyediting, but there really is a difference. You read proofs during proofreading. You edit copy during copyediting.

Proofreading is the process of reading **proofs** to correct mechanical errors made during writing or copyediting. A proof is a version of edited copy. It's considered final. If the copy has been placed in a designed page, it's a **page proof.** A page proof shows how the page will look when it's printed or photocopied.

Unlike copyediting, proofreading doesn't usually include checking facts or reorganization of ideas. You're correcting mistakes made when someone else typed the original copy or input corrections.

Someone else is key. You should never proofread your own copy. It's easy to miss something when you've been looking at it for a while.

Proofreader's Checklist

A variety of mistakes can creep in during copyediting—and afterwards, when the copy has been dropped into the pages. Whenever you make changes to copy, it should be proofread.

Check for the following:

Misspellings: Use a dictionary, a spell checker, and good sense. Take care not to change names without verification.

Punctuation errors: These include reversal of quotation marks (often caused by extra spacing) and missing periods.

Missing copy: Sometimes copy is accidentally left out, cut off, or moved during electronic "cutting and pasting."

Bad breaks: When a word breaks at the end of a line in an awkward way, readability is hampered.

Widows and orphans: A **widow** is a short line at the end of a paragraph appearing at the top of a page or column. An **orphan** is a short word, or part of a word, at the end of a paragraph, sitting on a line by itself. (Some people call this a widow too.)

Missing indents: Indents should occur at the beginning of paragraphs and as required in tables or charts.

Extra spaces: These sneak in between letters, words, or at the end of sentences. *Note:* You only need one space after the end punctuation of a sentence. The extra spacing is a leftover from the days of typewriters. Computers automatically allow enough space after end punctuation.

Errors in accompanying copy: Headlines and cutlines are often overlooked because of the concentration on stories.

Reading and Marking Proofs

One of the main goals of proofreading is to ensure that corrections made on a previous proof show up correctly on the current one. If you're doing all your copyediting on hard copy, it's easy enough to check one against the other.

Nowadays, however, there may be no hard copy of a previous phase showing corrections. In these cases, the proofreader just reads the current proof. This is called a **cold read.** You may do a cold read electronically or manually. If you do it electronically, you make the changes electronically at the same time.

If you're reading and marking changes on hard-copy proofs, use the copyediting symbols (p. 124). Write your corrections in the margins adjacent to the line in which they should occur. Draw a horizontal line to corrections if necessary (but don't cross lines). If there's more than one correction on a line, mark the corrections in the order in which they occur in the line. Separate these corrections by vertical lines.

Press Time

The oldest surviving copy of a newspaper printed in English was published in Amsterdam by a journalist who had lived in London for a few years. It begins with an apology: "The new tydings out of Italie are not yet com." Those words are spelled correctly for the time—1620. But the second page of the same issue has a glaring typo. It lists the date of publication as "The 2. of Decemember."

EXplore / EXpand / EXpress

1 **Explore Your World** Read several stories in a local or city paper. Do they seem complete? well organized? well written? Is there any editorializing? Are all opinions and controversial facts attributed? Do you notice any ways of handling copy that might be part of the newspaper's style?

2 **Expand Your Skills** Write a short article based on information from at least two sources. Copyedit the article on hard copy using copyediting symbols. Which resources were most helpful? Make the corrections and ask someone to proofread your copy against the previous hard copy. Check the proofreader's work. Try the same exercise completely electronically. Is there a difference in ease or quality of work between copyediting and proofreading electronically and manually? Which do you prefer? Why?

3 **Express Yourself** In your Journalist's Notebook, write what you imagine might be a copy editor's diary entry after finishing an issue. What kinds of things does the copy editor find most enjoyable or interesting about the job? most annoying? most difficult?

Design and Production

Design Basics

Design and Content headed out to meet the Readers.

"I'll lead the way," said Design. "They notice me first anyway."

"You can lead, but you have to lead them to me," replied Content.

"Let's go hand in hand!" both cried at once.

A rule often applied to design is "Form follows function." This means that the design of an item should suit its purpose. You already know that the purpose of a newspaper is to give readers content that they want and need. To suit that purpose, design is increasingly taking a leading role.

In part, this is the result of **desktop publishing.** Desktop publishing is the use of a desktop computer to write, edit, design, and prepare pages for publications.

The impact of technology on the entire process of newspaper publishing is mind-boggling, but particularly in design. At the heart of newspaper design, however, are goals and principles that should guide your overall vision and your everyday actions.

Press Time

The debut of the national newspaper *USA Today* in 1982 was met with some controversy. Critics thought it lacked substance. They compared it with fast food and dubbed it "McPaper." The response from the general public, however, was more favorable. Busy readers appreciated the colorful, news-at-a-glance style of the publication. Within a decade the paper became the largest daily in the United States in terms of circulation.

Goals of Newspaper Design

Today's readers prefer their news in colorful, visually appealing packages of quick-to-read, meaningful information.

You may be tempted to offer readers dazzling design that dizzies the senses. Avoid the temptation of "flash over substance" by maintaining a concentration on quality content. Your design should make the news easy to find, easy to read, and easy to understand.

To be effective, your design must accomplish three goals:

1. It must invite the reader into the paper with an attractive visual presentation.
2. It must lead the reader in an orderly way through the paper, drawing attention to content, pointing out its relative importance, and highlighting which content is related. This is usually accomplished with **entry points.** An entry point is a visual element that draws readers into a story or page.
3. It must assist the reader by making all content readable.

Basic Principles of Design

Meeting the goals of newspaper design takes creativity, skill, and experience. Keep these basic principles of design in mind:

Unity: Strive for a sense of wholeness—so each page looks different, yet all have the same visual tone, or feeling.

Consistency: Apply an identical design to elements that are identical; apply a similar design to elements that are similar.

Dominance: Use one visual focal point, or **dominant element,** on each page to serve as an entry point for readers as well as a center of visual interest.

Contrast: Use opposites in color, size, and shape to create emphasis and to distinguish one element from another.

Repetition: Repeat visual arrangements to create order.

Balance: Create a feeling of stability with a visually pleasing and dynamic distribution of elements on each page.

Measurement: Picas and Points

Most designers use a system of measurement based on two units of measure: **picas** and **points.** A pica is one-sixth of an inch; that is, there are 6 picas in one inch. The pica can be broken down further into points. One pica is equal to 12 points. So one inch equals 72 points. This might make it clearer:

1 inch = 6 picas
1 pica = 12 points
1 inch = 72 points

Overall dimensions of pages are usually measured in inches or centimeters. Designers use picas and points to measure type and the space between elements on a page. You might find a **pica stick** useful. It shows picas and inches.

Layout

Here's where you fit all the pieces together—stories, artwork, photos, and ads. The overall picture created is the newspaper's design.

Because you arrange, or lay out, the pieces of each page as you design your paper, the design stage is often called the **layout** stage. The resulting arrangement is also referred to as a layout.

Each item in a layout can be classified as one of three basic visual elements:

- **copy** or **text:** words
- **graphics** or **art:** photographs, illustrations, and devices such as lines, boxes, screens, charts, graphs, diagrams, maps, and arrows
- **white space:** empty (blank) areas

Page Elements

Thumb through any newspaper and you'll see elements that look familiar. Every newspaper contains similar page elements. To work productively on layouts, you need to understand the definitions, purpose, and placement of these elements:

nameplate or **flag:** copy (often combined with a graphic) that states the name of the newspaper in large bold letters across the front page. It includes the volume number and issue number, publication date, and city and state where the paper is published.
masthead: a boxed item that gives important information about the newspaper (p. 109)
teaser: boxed copy that promotes stories inside the issue
index: copy that lists the page numbers on which each section starts
column: a vertical section of printed copy in a layout
leg: a vertical column of copy, referred to by its length in inches (for example, "4-inch leg")
headline: a very brief description of a story printed in larger type, usually above the story (p. 64)
deck: one level of a headline
subhead: a miniheadline that indicates what the next section of copy contains
standing head: a headline for a regular item in each issue of a newspaper
byline: a credit that tells who wrote a story
dateline: a line of copy that identifies the place where the news occurred

jumpline: a line of copy that indicates the page on which a story continues

refer: a line of copy that points readers to a related story elsewhere in the issue

cutline or **caption:** information that accompanies a photograph or other graphic (p. 70)

photo credit: a line of copy that identifies the photographer of a particular photo

jumphead: a brief, one- or two-word headline on a page that shows a reader where to start reading a jumped story again (p. 121)

pull quote: a quote taken from a story and arranged as a graphic in the layout of the story

folio: a page number. The folio often includes the name and section of the paper as well.

gutter: white space that separates columns and facing pages

screen: a shaded area. The lightness or darkness of a screen is measured in percentages. A 10-percent screen is light, whereas a 50-percent screen is fairly dark.

rule: a thin vertical or horizontal line that serves to accent or separate elements. Its width is measured in points (p. 136).

initial cap or **drop cap:** a large capital letter of the opening word in a story, which serves as a graphic and an entry point (p. 135)

mugshot or **headshot:** a photo that shows only the shoulders and head of a person

infographic: a graphic that presents statistical information, such as a map, chart, diagram, or time line

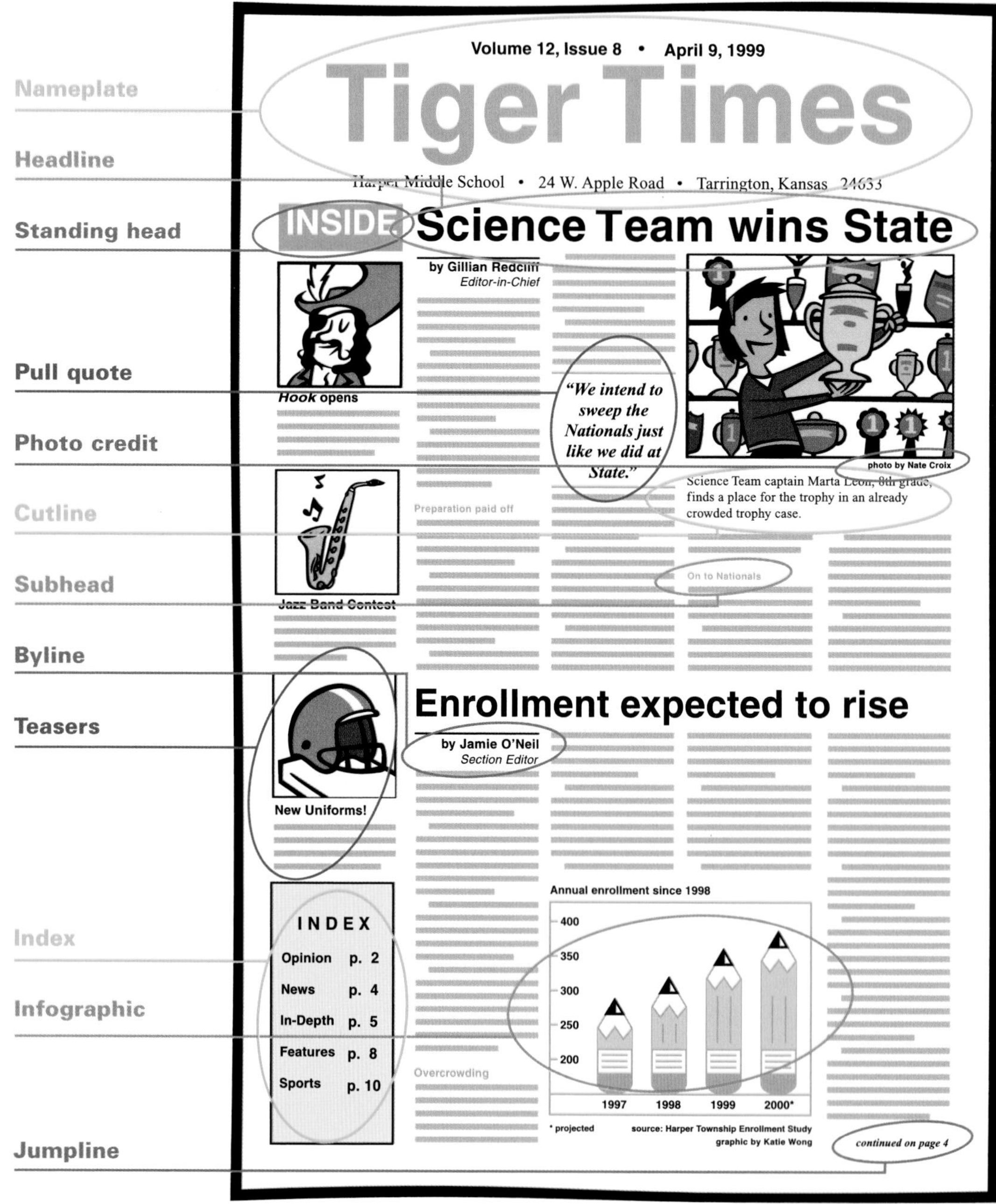
Nameplate
Headline
Standing head
Pull quote
Photo credit
Cutline
Subhead
Byline
Teasers
Index
Infographic
Jumpline
Volume 12, Issue 8 • April 9, 1999
Tiger Times
Harper Middle School • 24 W. Apple Road • Tarrington, Kansas 24633
INSIDE
Science Team wins State
by Gillian Redcliff
Editor-in-Chief
Hook opens
"We intend to sweep the Nationals just like we did at State."
photo by Nate Croix
Science Team captain Marta Leon, 8th grade, finds a place for the trophy in an already crowded trophy case.
Preparation paid off
On to Nationals
Jazz Band Contest
Enrollment expected to rise
by Jamie O'Neil
Section Editor
New Uniforms!
INDEX
Opinion p. 2
News p. 4
In-Depth p. 5
Features p. 8
Sports p. 10
Annual enrollment since 1998
400
350
300
250
200
1997
1998
1999
2000*
Overcrowding
* projected
source: Harper Township Enrollment Study
graphic by Katie Wong
continued on page 4

logo: an identification mark, usually consisting of copy combined with a graphic

spot color: one color applied in strategic places on a page

clip art: ready-made graphics available for use free of charge or for a small fee

icon: a graphic symbol

bleed: the running of a photo or other graphic through the external margin and off a page

overprint: the printing of one item on top of another

bullet: a centered dot that calls attention to a line of copy or sets off items in a list

facing pages: two inside pages that face each other but that are not usually printed on the same sheet of paper

spread: a set of facing pages

centerspread or **double-truck:** a spread in the center of a newspaper, printed as one sheet of paper

internal margin: a consistent margin of white space between copy and graphics. It's usually one pica in width (p. 136).

external margin: a frame of white space around the layout marked by the outside edge of at least one block of copy or graphic

fold: the middle of a page where large-format newspapers are folded

Press Time

The term *tabloid* came out of the pharmaceutical industry of the late 1800s. It referred to easily digested medicines. The first American tabloid newspaper, New York's *Daily News,* was founded in 1919. By 1925 the paper was selling a million copies a day. Tabloids were very popular for two main reasons. Their reduced size made them easier than broadsheets to read on trains or trolleys. And their content included many photographs and sensationalized stories, which were "easy to digest."

Format

The first thing you face during layout is a blank page. The physical size of this page is known as the **format.**

Most city newspapers use the **broadsheet** format. This is approximately 14 by 22 inches.

On the other hand, school papers are most likely to use a **tabloid** format, which is approximately 11 by 17 inches. Some school papers use a **news-magazine** format, which is 8 1/2 by 11 inches, or standard letter-size.

Grids

A **grid** is a pattern of lines that forms a base on which you can place elements. Vertical column lines show the column width and space between columns. Horizontal lines are typically at one-inch increments.

The format you choose will determine, in part, the width of your columns. A broadsheet usually has six columns, a tabloid four or five columns, and a news magazine two or three columns.

Most newspapers stick to one standard column width. For variety, a slightly wider or narrower width may be used for some stories. A general rule is that the wider columns go on the bottom of the pages. Otherwise, they appear to smash the smaller columns below. Feel free to be somewhat flexible with your column widths—but flex within your grid.

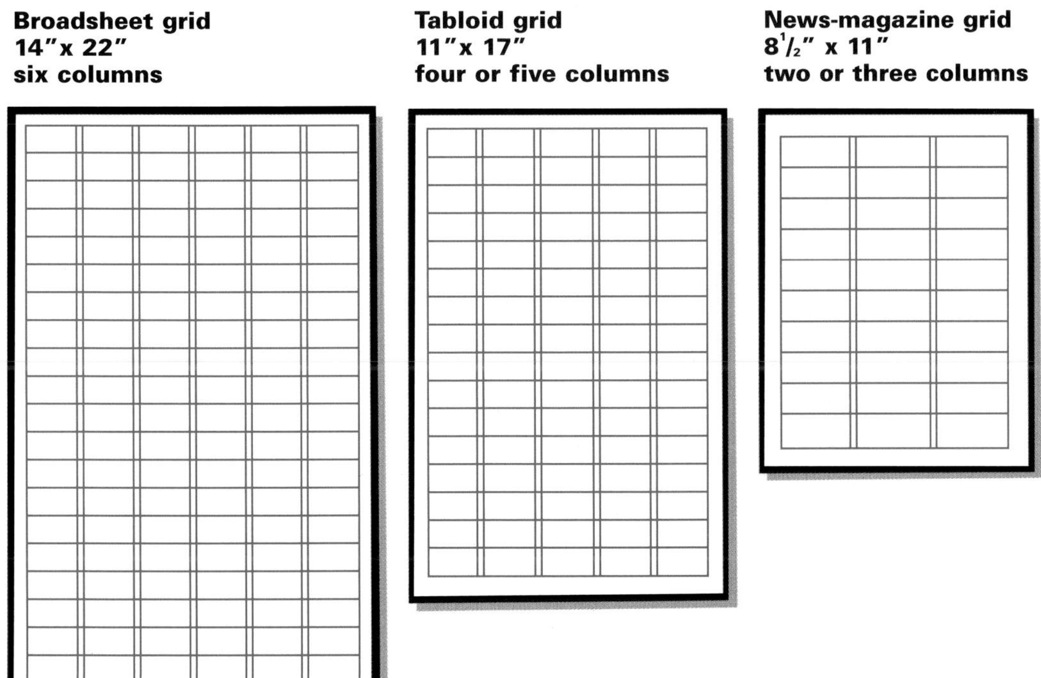

Thumbnails and Dummies

Rarely do designers lay out a page without first making design sketches. Start with **thumbnails**—small, rough representations of pages. From your thumbnails, prepare a **dummy** for each page. Dummies are the actual size of finished pages and show where all page elements will appear.

For convenience, use **grid sheets** to create your dummies. Grid sheets are paper, the size of the newspaper format, that are lined with light-colored grid marks. Light-colored lines allow you to see the grid but prevent you from getting grid lines confused with pencil lines as you sketch your dummy. You may have your printer provide grid sheets or print them yourselves from your computer. Some designers do their dummies right on the computer.

TIPS Making Dummies

- Show a photo or graphic as a white box with a large *X* and a label inside the box.
- Show an ad as a white box with one diagonal line and a label inside the box.
- Show a story as a box with one vertical line running down each column leg and a label inside the box. Some designers connect the bottom of the line in one column with the top of the line in the next column to show how readers' eyes move. Draw an arrow at the end of the line in the last column of the story. An alternative to the vertical line is a series of horizontal lines to indicate copy in each column.
- If you use computer software to prepare your dummies, you can use screened blocks to indicate photos or stories. You can also use nonsense copy to stand in for copy. Nonsense copy

should have *no meaning.* It's a series of letters that look like words and sentences. Keep a document of nonsense copy for this purpose.

- Use a series of *X*s or squiggly lines to indicate headlines, cutlines, bylines, photo credits, folios, and other similar lines of copy.

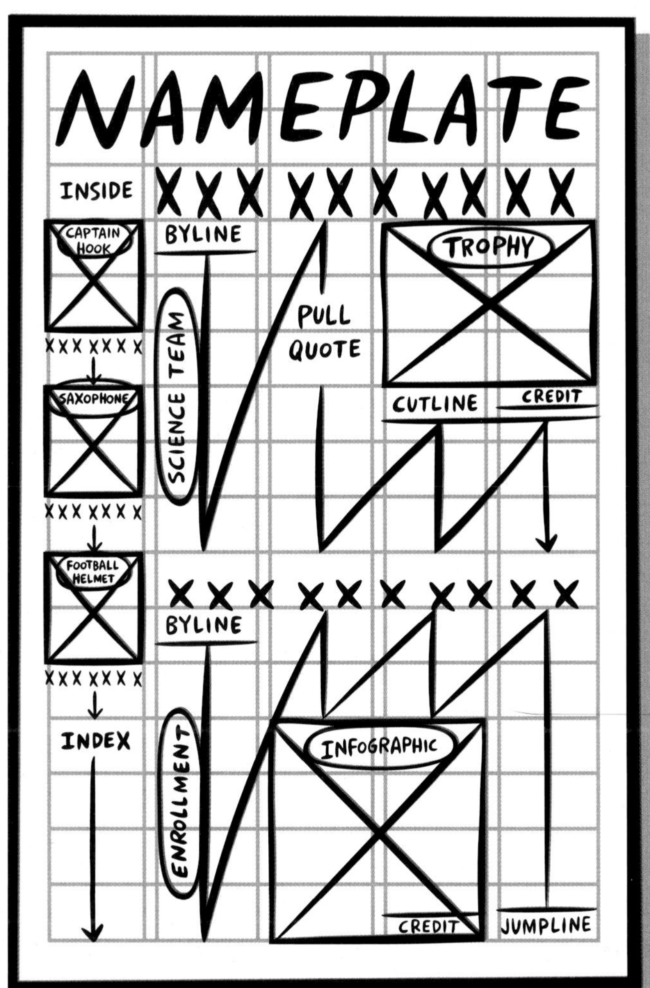

Tabloid dummy, based on the top thumbnail on the opposite page; see page 140 for the finished, printed page

Modular Design

The most common way to package news is by using **modular design.** In modular design, you lay out the page in square or rectangular units.

Each unit is a minilayout. It consists of all the visual elements—copy, graphics, and white space—that make up a particular story. Each modular unit has a dominant element (p. 136). One unit is the dominant element on the page or centerspread.

A typical modular unit for a story might contain story copy, a headline, a byline, subheads, a pull quote, a photo, a cutline, and a photo credit.

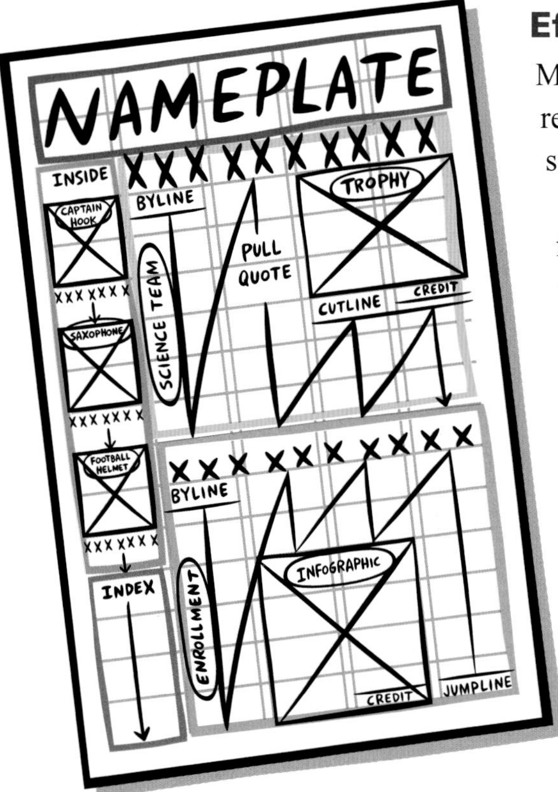

Effective and Efficient Design

Modular design is effective because it enables readers to get all of a story in one package and see sidebars packaged alongside.

Modular design is efficient because it's flexible. You can pick up and move whole units around. Since each unit stands alone, modular design also allows you to have different numbers of columns for different modular units. Like most layouts, laying out pages in a modular design is best done on a grid.

Standout Layouts

Many challenges arise in laying out a well-designed page. Keep in mind the basic design principles and the goals of newspaper design. Experiment and learn from experience. Borrow from papers with standout layouts. Most will exhibit these strategies.

Overall Arrangement

- Place the most important news at the top of the page, with less important news toward the bottom. Another convention is to put the most important story in the top right corner.
- Include at least two stories and one or two graphics per page. (The news-magazine format may allow only one story per page.)
- Avoid having all jumped stories end up on the same page (p. 121).
- Group smaller stories, such as news briefs, together.
- Place the dominant element in the upper half of your grid. Fit other elements around it. A secondary visual focal point can go in the lower half of the grid.
- Use a large photo or other graphic as a dominant element only if it's very interesting and of good quality.
- Design a centerspread as if it were one page. Place facing pages side by side during layout to ensure that they complement each other. Make sure a dominant element ties the pages together.
- Make sure the entry point of each story is clear to readers.
- Establish standards for leg length. Seven inches is a standard maximum; two inches is a standard minimum.
- Avoid widows and orphans (p. 130).

Bylines and Headlines

- Place bylines at the beginning of a story.
- Make the size of the headline reflect the importance of the story. Reserve large headlines for school-shattering news.
- Make sure you only have one dominant headline per page.
- Avoid small, wordy headlines. They lose their effectiveness.
- Keep headlines that run across three columns or more to one deck.
- Leave more space above a headline than below.
- Avoid **tombstoning,** which is the placing of two headlines side by side. You can sometimes get away with it if one story is boxed and the headlines are different type sizes.
- Never separate a headline from its story with a photo or with any other graphic.
- Run only large headlines across the entire width of the paper.
- Use a kicker, tripod, or hammerhead (p. 65) for variety in headlines, but no more than one of each type on a page.

Subheads, Pull Quotes, and Initial Caps

- Avoid placing a subhead or a pull quote next to a cutline unless the contrast is dramatic enough to distinguish between the two.
- Use a pull quote and subheads to help spice up and break up a long story.
- Keep your subheads to one line.
- If you use initial caps, use them only on feature pages and only to draw attention to the beginning of the most important story on the page. This device loses its effect if it's overused.

Graphics

- Make it obvious which photos and graphics go with which stories.
- Vary arrangement of copy and graphics. Run columns of copy in a U-shape or an L-shape around a graphic. Wrap copy around small or odd-shaped graphics.
- If you wrap copy around a graphic in the middle of the story, don't leave half a sentence on one side of the graphic and half on the other.
- Avoid having a photo and another graphic directly next to each other, even if they're related. Separate them with copy.
- When you bleed a graphic across the gutter between the pages of a centerspread, keep in mind that your newspaper might have a fold that could cause a crease in the graphic.

Margins and White Space

- Leave white space to avoid crowding the page, but keep the space to the outside margins of the page. That way, you can avoid **trapped white space,** an empty block of space boxed into the middle of the page.
- Leave a consistent internal margin between all graphics (including photos) and copy. Typically this is at least one pica wide.
- Leave at least two picas of space between the copy of one story and the headline of another story beneath it.
- When you box a story, leave at least one pica of space between the border and the copy.

Color

- Use color wisely. If you use color on the front page, you can use it on the back page too at no extra cost because it's the same piece of paper. But don't overdo it. Use color to accent only the most important items on the page.
- If you decide to use color as a border around photos, bear in mind that each color will be printed on a different press run, or at different times, on the page. A slight shifting could cause problems with **registration,** the correct positioning of elements in a printed image.

Alignment

- Align elements vertically in each column or modular unit. **Alignment** refers to any line created as a result of the way page elements are arranged.
- Align elements horizontally across the top of columns and at the top and bottom of pages. That's **cross alignment.**
- Align the **baseline,** or bottom, of lines of type next to each other. That's **base alignment.**

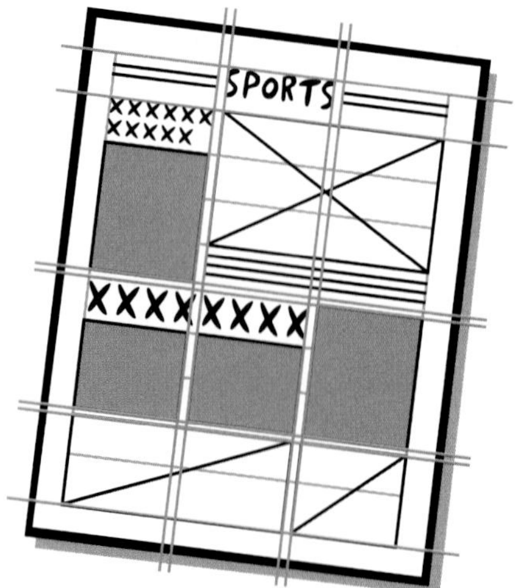

Typography

Have you ever looked a letter in its face and wondered about its width and weight? How bold!

Typography is the way printed letters are handled on a page. It's a major influence in establishing the look and feel of any publication.

Typography is also key to accomplishing the goals of newspaper design (p.135). It can add immensely to the visual appeal of a page, helps to lead readers through the paper, and is a major factor in making content readable.

Understanding some basic typography concepts and terms will help you as you work with the rest of the design staff.

Talking Type

If someone said, "Let's use 10/12 Helvetica Condensed Bold for our cutlines," would you know what they were talking about? Knowing how to talk type can speed up and clarify communication among designers. The language of typography is simple once you get to know a few basic terms:

character: a type letter (such as an *A*) or letterform (such as a hyphen)

typeface: a design of a complete set of type characters, specified by a name, such as Arial or Garamond

font: a complete set of characters in one size and style of a typeface, such as 12-point Gill Sans Italic. Type size is measured in points (p. 136). Type style refers to the weight, width, and posture of a character.

family: fonts closely related in style

Gill Sans Font Family

Gill Sans	Gill Sans Bold Condensed
Gill Sans Italic	***Gill Sans Bold Italic***
Gill Sans Light	**Gill Sans Extra Bold**
Gill Sans Light Italic	**Gill Sans Ultra Bold**
Gill Sans Condensed	**Gill Sans Ultra Bold Condensed**
Gill Sans Bold	

weight: the visual width of the strokes that make up each letter. *Light, medium, demibold, bold,* and *extrabold* are terms used to describe the weight of a typeface.

width: the horizontal measure of a type character. *Condensed* and *extended* are terms used to describe the width of a typeface.

posture: the slant of a letter. A right slant is referred to by the term *italic* or *oblique.* An upright posture is referred to as *roman.*
leading or **linespacing:** the space between the baseline (p. 150) of one line of type and the baseline of the next, measured in points. This copy is set at 12 points with 4 points of leading "base-to-base." Designers say it's set "12 on 16," which is written as 12/16. Most newspaper copy is set 10/12.
letterspacing: space between letters in a line of copy
reverse print: light type on a dark background
serif: a class of type with small "feet" or strokes at the end of most letters. Serif typefaces include Garamond, Palatino, and City.
sans serif: a class of type without serifs. Sans serif typefaces include Optima, Helvetica, and Gill Sans.
script: a class of type that resembles handwriting. Linoscript, Boulevard, and Kuenstler are script typefaces.
novelty: a class of type that reflects a particular mood or historic period. Novelty typefaces include Lemonade, Arnold Bocklin, and Wilhelm Klingspor Gottisch.

Garamond

City

Palatino

Optima

Helvetica

Gill Sans

Lemonade

Arnold Bocklin

Wilhelm Klingspor Gottisch

Linoscript

Boulevard

Kuenstler

Body Type and Display Type

This paragraph is set in New Times Roman, 12/16. The head is Dom Casual Bold, 20/20. If these fonts were switched, this paragraph would be much longer and would look ridiculous. Not only that, but it would be hard to read. Remember the goals of newspaper design!

When it comes to choosing typefaces, choose a font that's easy to read for **body type**—type for columns of copy. Body type is usually a serif typeface. That's because the serifs form subtle lines at the top and bottom of the characters to guide the reader.

Sans serif and novelty fonts are often used for **display type**—type for headlines, bylines, cutlines, and other special uses. Display type can impart a mood or specific meaning tied to the content. For example, if you're doing a centerspread feature on comic book heroes, you might use a typeface with a comic book style.

Press Time

The typeface used to print the American Declaration of Independence was created by a British typeface designer, William Caslon. Caslon first began designing type for the Oxford University Press in 1720. His typefaces achieved great popularity throughout Europe and America. Another renowned typeface designer of the 1700s was Giambattista Bodoni. He began his career in 1758 working in the Vatican's printing house. Bodoni's elegant typefaces are still in frequent use today. He's sometimes called the father of modern typography.

Type Alignment

Readability assumes all importance again when it comes to type alignment (p. 150). Some alignments are more readable than others.

Type set **flush left** is easiest to read. Flush-left alignment provides a vertical line at the left margin of copy. Readers use the line as a point of return when they reach the end of each line of copy. Flush-left alignment is commonly used for body type as well as headlines and cutlines. This paragraph is set flush left.

This paragraph is set **flush right.** Flush-right alignment creates a line on the right margin. It's best left to special uses, such as bylines, or cutlines set to the left side of a photo.

Many papers use **justified** alignment. This paragraph is justified. Justified alignment creates a line on both the right and left margins of a column. It's not as easy to read as flush left, but it's preferable to **force-justified** alignment. That can result in gaping holes that create rivers of white space between words and letters in a column of copy.

Centered alignment provides no line on the right or left margin.
It's often used for invitations and ads, set one sentence per line.
In large blocks of copy it's not very readable.
The only way you can show paragraph breaks is with a blank line.

Centered copy should look centered—not like flush-left copy that's
out of whack. You may have to adjust line breaks so the lines form
a pleasing, readable arrangement from top to bottom as well as
from side to side. As you might have guessed,
these last two paragraphs are centered.

Top-Notch Typography

For young designers, nothing is quite so exciting as playing with type. Try to be conservative with typography at first. Be consistent and keep readability in mind. You'll come up with top-notch typography if you pay attention to these guiding principles.

Type Style

- Use just a few fonts. Stick with *no more than* three or four: one each for body type, headlines, pull quotes, and cutlines. All but the body type might be in the same font family.
- For the best readability, use a serif typeface for body type. For contrast, use the same serif typeface for headlines and subheads and a sans serif typeface for other display type. Or for greater contrast, use a sans serif typeface for all display type.
- For a special feature story, you may choose a headline typeface different from your standard one to strike a mood or convey a specific message.
- Avoid script and novelty typefaces for body type. Even for display type, they should be used sparingly.

Leading

- Be consistent in your leading throughout the paper.
- As a general rule, for point sizes 8–14, add 2 points of leading; for point sizes 16–24, add 4 points; for point sizes 26–36, add 6 points.

Type Size

- Body type should be the same size throughout the paper, generally no smaller than 9 points and no larger than 12 points.
- Make headlines no smaller than 14 points. Use these small-sized heads only over short blocks of copy such as news briefs.
- Make headlines no larger than 48 points, except on centerspreads.
- Set bylines and cutlines slightly larger than body type. Or make them smaller and bold.
- Pull quotes should be larger than the body type for emphasis, but not so large that they compete with headlines.

Type Formatting

- Avoid all caps! Copy set in all caps is almost always harder to read. And *never* set a script typeface in all caps.
- In body type, use bold and italics for emphasis only. Use italic in body copy only as your stylebook advises (p. 122).
- You can use all bold—and in small doses, all italic—for display type but not for body type.

Type Alignment

- Be consistent in type alignment. All headlines and subheads should have the same alignment. All bylines should have the same alignment. All columns and cutlines should have the same alignment, and all pull quotes should have the same alignment.
- Set type horizontally, never vertically.

Column Width

- Keep line width in the readable range. Use this formula: Double the point size to get a number representing the maximum width. Subtract eight picas from that number to get the minimum width. Add four picas to the minimum to get the optimum width. For a line of 10-point type: 10 x 2 = 20; – 8 = 12; + 4 = 16; so the range is 12–20 picas, with 16 the optimum width.
- Use the same column width throughout a story. Use no more than two different column widths within your publication. These should be clearly different.

Indenting

- Use an indent rather than a blank line to signal a new paragraph.
- Make indents consistent and apparent: one pica is sufficient.
- Don't indent the first paragraph of a story or the first paragraph under a subhead. This is a common design no-no.

Overprinting and Reverse Type

- Avoid using reverse print with serif typefaces or in large blocks of copy. Save it for small standing heads or bylines.
- Use screens of gray or color behind type sparingly, especially with body type. Use only very light screens (10–15 percent) and only sans serif type (the serifs get lost in a screen).
- Avoid printing type over a patterned background or photograph, even ghosted (faintly printed) photographs.

Graphics

Since prehistoric times, people have used graphics to communicate.

Some scientists believe that ancient cave paintings were intended to explain how and where to hunt. The use of graphics has come a long way in a few million years. Possibilities for creating graphics today seem endless. Computer programs allow you to manipulate images in amazing ways. Lines, boxes, color, and screens appear with the click of a mouse and a few keystrokes.

Reasons for using graphics, however, are more defined. The primary function of newspaper graphics is to communicate. They can often explain what words can't. They can emphasize a point, show comparisons, and convey the expression in someone's face.

A secondary function is to add visual variety that draws readers into a page. Photographs, illustrations, charts, diagrams, and maps are typically more inviting than columns of copy.

To Emphasize and Distinguish

A common use for graphics is to emphasize a page element or to distinguish one element from another. In this sense, they may serve as entry points (p. 135). Keep these guidelines in mind:

- Graphics for emphasis should contrast with surrounding copy.
- If you're using an illustration for emphasis, say to highlight a sidebar, use one with a bright color or a strong black-and-white contrast. An overall gray tone will blend in with the copy.
- Your illustration doesn't need to be big, but if it's small make sure it's executed with bold, clean lines. In general, the smaller your graphic, the less detail you should use.
- If you're using a photograph for emphasis, especially if it's the dominant element, make it large. Or make it a color photo or a high-contrast black-and-white photo.
- If you're using graphic devices such as rules, boxes, and screens to distinguish one page element from another, keep a tight rein. A one- or two-point rule or box border is enough. Limit yourself to one screened element on a page.

To Communicate and Clarify

Graphics, especially photographs, can communicate in obvious or subtle ways. A photo of a young girl lifting weights may say that the girl is training to gain strength. It may also say that girls use weights to gain strength just as boys do. Be conscious of what your photos are saying and their power to elicit strong emotions.

If a graphic is supposed to clarify a concept, it must be especially clear itself. Use simple illustrations rather than photographs, which have more room for interpretation. Label the parts of the graphic for extra clarity or add a brief cutline. If you can, use color to highlight important parts of the graphic.

Infographics

Infographics, such as graphs and tables, are used to clarify concepts in a story. They should *not* be used just to add variety or to present information that could be given in a sentence or two.

Follow these rules when you use an infographic:

- Make it large enough to be readable.
- Use a strong, meaningful piece of art.
- Label or add details to parts of the graphic by drawing a line to a short bit of copy. This copy is referred to as a **callout.**
- Give it a headline.
- Credit the source.
- Credit the artist.

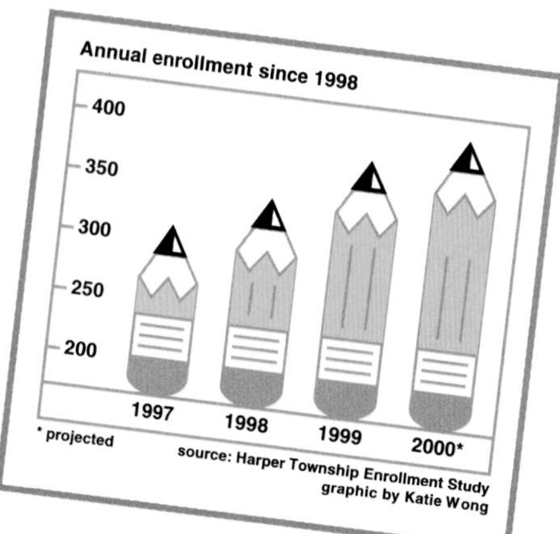

To Unify and Identify

Repetition and consistency in the use of graphics go a long way toward establishing unity and identity in a newspaper. You may repeat a specific graphic with a standing head (p. 138). Or you may always place a rule over a byline. By consistent repetition of these little things, you create your paper's visual personality.

Establish a tone to standardized graphics. Choose a tone appropriate to each section and maintain it. Graphics in your news section may be sophisticated, while graphics in your features section are more jazzy.

To unify the graphics throughout, pick one visual style. It might be one that resembles an art medium, such as woodcut or pen and ink. Surprises are great—but if you want to establish an identity, be consistent in your use of graphics.

Handling Photos

If you use desktop publishing software to create your pages, you'll find a **scanner** useful, especially for handling photos. A scanner works something like a photocopying machine, except that it converts a physical object or image into an electronic image. You can scan a pencil and use it as a graphic! You can also scan photographs and then lay them into your pages on the computer.

If you don't have a scanner, ask your printer to scan your photograph or convert it to a **halftone** and place it on the page. A halftone is a photograph made of your photograph, shot through a special screen that converts the original image into a series of dots. The dots blend together into the photographic image when viewed from a normal distance. If you pull out a magnifying glass, you can see the dots.

Press Time

During the Civil War, Mathew Brady organized a corps of photographers who followed the armies to record the war firsthand. But Brady's photographs were not widely seen until much later. Newspapers of the day did not yet have the technology to print photographs. Instead they sent artists to the combat zones to sketch realistic battle scenes. The sketches were reproduced as engravings and printed in the newspapers. In 1873 the *New York Daily Graphic* was the first newspaper to publish a photograph. It was of New York's Steinway Hall.

Ad Layout

Lay out an ad that sells, sells, sells! Get free admission into the Hall of Ad-Layout Fame.

Two main types of ads appear in newspapers: **classified ads** and **display ads.** Most school papers don't run classified ads. Display ads, however, may make up 50 percent of your newspaper space.

A classified ad is a short block of copy placed by an individual or business trying to sell a service or product. Classifieds run in straight columns of copy. Subheads identify their classification, for example, items to trade, or help wanted. Very little design goes into classified ads.

A display ad is an eye-catching ad placed by a business or organization. Display ads are larger and include more elements.

Designing display ads is a challenging part of the layout process. But it can be rewarding—in terms of your paper's final appearance and the appreciation of advertisers.

Dimensions of Ads

Classified ads are sold by the word. They're set like body type, sometimes smaller by one point size. Display ads are usually sold by the **column inch** or by a fraction of a page: 1/8, 1/4, 1/2, and full-page. A column inch is the space in your paper that is one inch high and the width of your standard column.

The smallest ad you might lay out will probably be two column inches; most will be bigger. The horizontal and vertical dimensions of ads are flexible: A four-inch ad could be two inches high and two columns wide, four inches high and one column wide, or one inch high and four columns wide.

Four-inch ads

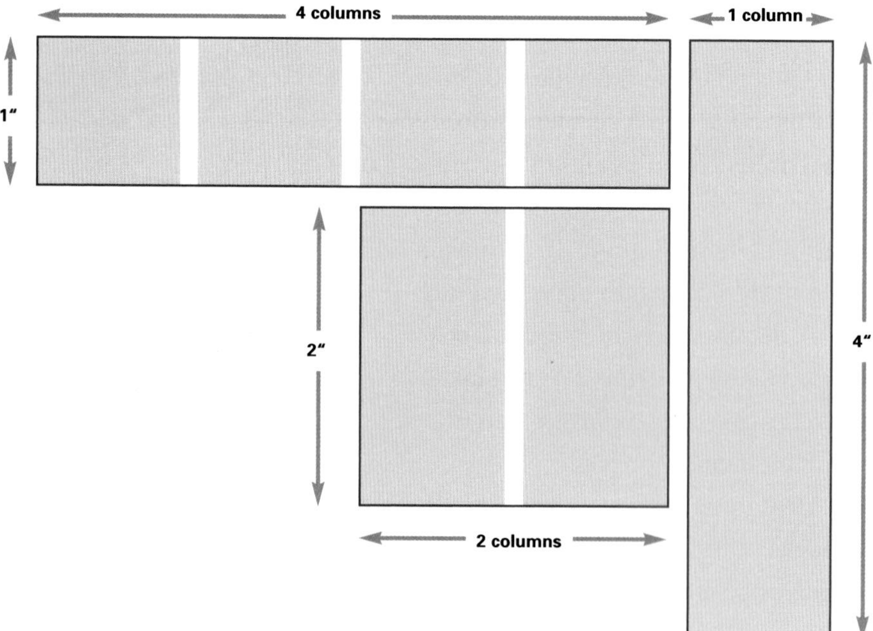

Elements of a Display Ad

Most display ads contain the following elements:

- **benefit heads:** headline and subhead that grab the reader's attention and explain the benefit of responding to the ad
- **copy** or **text:** words; includes the **pitch** (information about the product or service) followed by the **close** (calls readers to action); may include a **slogan** (a short, catchy phrase that identifies the product with the advertiser); may also include a caption for the graphic, if necessary
- **graphic** or **art:** photographs, illustrations, and devices such as lines, boxes, screens, charts, graphs, diagrams, maps, and arrows; typography as art may serve as a graphic in an ad
- **white space:** empty (blank) areas
- **identification:** the advertiser's name, address, phone, and other contact details

Ads with Impact

Arrangement of the elements in an ad varies. In most cases, you'll be following the advertiser's **specs,** or specifications (p. 214). These spell out exactly what the advertiser wants to say and how the ad should look. If the ad looks awful, offer to improve it. But get the advertiser's approval first.

Some advertisers will give you ads that are **camera-ready,** or ready to be placed as they are. Or an advertiser may just give you a graphic to use. This is called a **slick.**

When you have to design from scratch, follow the principles for page layout and typography. In addition, here are a few tips to help you create ads with impact.

TIPS Ads with Impact

- Include a graphic as your dominant element, preferably a photo or an illustration of the product.
- Use high-quality art. If you don't have a computer illustration program, use clip art or use type as a graphic element.
- Use white space to call attention to important copy.
- Use sans serif typefaces for smaller point sizes.
- Avoid heavy or fancy borders. A one- or two-point rule is good.
- If two ads are to be placed next to each other, use different typefaces or add a light screen to one.

Placing Ads

Ads are often placed on the page layout before other copy. You may think that the news is more important than the advertising. But by placing ads first, you'll make sure you have room for all the ads that were bought.

Ads can be placed anywhere in the paper. It's best, however, to avoid any advertising on the front page and on the editorial pages. You may also wish to rule out ads on your centerspread.

Most designers place ads in one of two ways:

- arranged in an L-shape, anchored in the lower corner
- placed in modular units, like stories

TIPS Placing Ads

- Place large ads and those with heavy graphics on the bottom of pages, preferably in the right-hand corner.
- Ads of similar dimensions may be stacked in a column, but keep them to the outside of the page. Advertisers don't like to see their ads buried in the gutter.
- As you're placing ads, think about variation in dimension. Avoid a line of ads the same size and shape.
- Don't place ads of competing clients next to each other. They won't like it.
- If you run out of ads to fill a modular unit, insert an ad that promotes an event at your school, advertises topics to be covered in the next issue, or advertises buying an ad.
- Keep at least one pica of space between all ads. Keep two picas of space between ads and stories.

Paste-up

Finally! You're done with the layout! Now you have to place all the elements on the pages and get them ready for printing. This could take awhile . . . .

The dummies you create during layout form the blueprint for building the pages. This building stage is called **paste-up.** Traditionally, paste-up involves using glue or wax to paste the visual elements onto paper. Most schools now use desktop publishing programs for paste-up.

Just as the pages you worked on during the layout stage were called layouts, the pages you finish during paste-up are called paste-ups.

Some schools use a **modem** to send their paste-ups electronically to a printer. A modem is a device that converts information into signals that can be sent and received over phone lines.

From Paste-up to Printer

These are the typical steps to prepare for and complete paste-up. A brief overview of what happens at the printer is included.

1. The design editor works with the editor-in-chief, section editors, and business manager to determine space needs for the current issue. The business manager, editor-in-chief, and design editor determine how much space is needed for ads and how much remains for the stories (p. 210).

2. The design editor makes assignments for page layout.
3. Designers prepare thumbnails and dummies for their assigned pages. They may do them on paper or the computer.
4. Designers paste up the pages according to the dummies. If your staff has not yet entered the age of computer publishing, all page elements are physically pasted or applied with wax onto the blank page.

   At this time, photos are either scanned into the layout or marked for sending to the printer. Photos are marked on the back and in the corresponding place on the correct newspaper page. That way the printer knows where to place them.
5. Paste-ups are printed out or photocopied for proofreading. Then corrections are made.
6. Final pages are sent to the printer or photocopier.
7. If your newspaper is printed at a print shop, your paste-ups are photographed with a special camera that creates a film negative of your pages. The film negative is used to make positive printing plates to print your paper. Some printers output film directly from the electronic files of your pages.
8. The printed paper is assembled and bound. Some news magazines have a **saddle-stitch binding,** staples down the center of all facing pages to hold the pages together.

Signatures

If you publish a broadsheet, tabloid, or news magazine with pages that aren't stapled together, you may wonder why your paper must be printed in multiples of four pages. That's because of **signatures.** A signature is a printed page after it's been folded for binding.

Most newspapers have no formal binding other than a fold. Each signature in a newspaper has four pages. These are fitted in a pattern inside each other.

A saddle-stitched news magazine may have 8- or 16-page signatures. The pages are folded, cut, and "stitched."

4-page signatures for 8-page tabloid

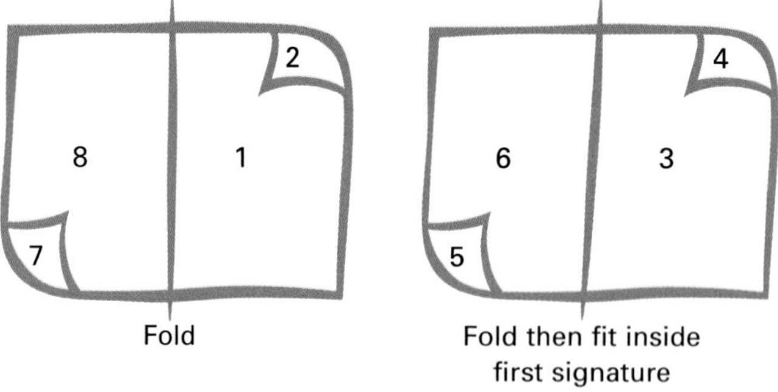

8-page signature for 8-page news magazine

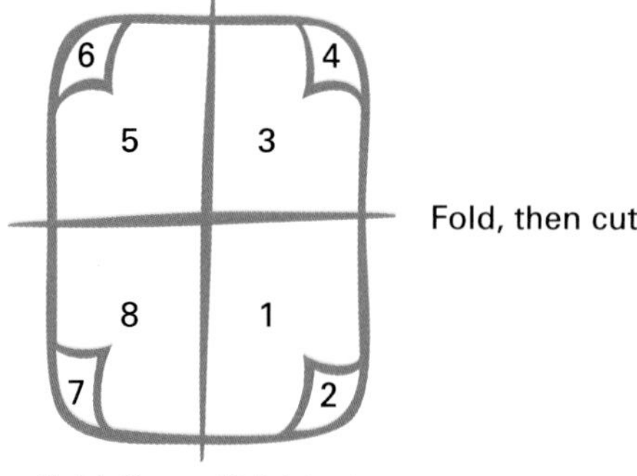

Design and Production Guide

Achieving a unified design is tricky when your newspaper has eight or more pages laid out by several students. Everyone wants to add their own special touches. Or the deadline is approaching and it seems no one has time to add anything special.

Once the design is completed, you have to make sure the pages are pasted-up and prepared properly for printing or photocopying. That process can be tricky too, especially with complicated layouts.

This is why the design staff should follow a guide for design and production that sets the rules for how elements will appear on the page. It also specifies how to prepare pages for reproduction.

You might include your design and production guide as a separate part of your newspaper's stylebook (p. 122). However you produce your guide, distribute it widely. Make multiple copies and scatter them around the production area. If a change is made to one of the rules, update *all* copies.

Press Time

German printers traditionally set their type in an elaborate script typeface. Members of the artistic movement known as the Bauhaus, founded in Germany in 1919, challenged this tradition. Bauhaus member Herbert Bayer designed simple, easy-to-read sans serif typefaces for use in the graphic arts. The new typefaces were streamlined in accordance with the Bauhaus ideal: "Form follows function." The nondecorative style was not welcome at first, but greater demands for readable display type in advertising helped popularize the new typographical trend.

1 **Explore Your World** Look through several newspapers and pick out the layouts you like best. Do they demonstrate the basic design principles? Do they accomplish the goals of newspaper design? Do they follow the guidelines for standout layouts, effective typography, and graphics? Do the ads have impact?

2 **Expand Your Skills** Make thumbnails or dummies of the layouts you found. How might you incorporate what you like about these layouts into your school paper using the skills and tools you have? How might you change these layouts with different typography and graphics?

3 **Express Yourself** Design a page that expresses your personality. Write copy about yourself and include graphics you create or find. Include an ad or two that promote something about yourself. Make a dummy or paste-up of your page and put it in your Journalist's Notebook.

Photojournalism

Photo Coverage

Photographs may be only two-dimensional, but they can make a story three-dimensional.

Photojournalism is not just taking pictures; it's telling the news through photographs. Like reporters, photojournalists, or news photographers, must have a nose for news. They must also have the skill to show news, accurately and objectively, through photographs.

The ways photos are used vary: Some stand alone as a story with a cutline and others are part of a photo essay (p. 71). Most photographs, however, accompany stories, so they must coordinate well with those stories. To accomplish this, you'll need to be prepared—not only for spontaneous photo opportunities but for more formally arranged photo sessions, or **shoots.**

First, you need to understand why photographs are used. Understanding the functions photos serve will guide the success of your photo coverage.

Functions of Photographs

Photographs serve several functions in newspapers. All are important, but communication is the most important function. Unless a photograph communicates something newsworthy, it's not photojournalism.

Communication

A photograph can communicate general information very quickly. For example, a photo of a student sweeping up after a dance tells readers this is one of the chores that have to be done after a dance. The cutline provides specific information (p. 70). It identifies the student and may explain that the chore falls to members of the dance committee.

Photos may communicate emotions as well as facts. They inform and express. The student's face and body posture, for example, may express disgust with the clean-up chore.

Mood too can be communicated in photographs. For example, you can convey the nostalgia at the end of a school year in a shot of the school grounds at sunset.

Credibility

A photograph makes whatever is pictured seem more real and true. It lends credibility to the story. People are more inclined to believe what they see than what they read.

Visual Appeal

Photographs are visual magnets, drawing readers into a page or a story. For this reason photos often serve as entry points (p. 135).

Part of a photograph's visual appeal is the variety it adds to a layout. The contrast between a photo and copy is exciting and eye-catching. That's why a photograph is usually the dominant element on a page or spread.

Vitality

A photograph adds life—vitality—to a story in a way no illustration can match. Even a mugshot (p. 139) can do wonders. It makes readers feel as though the person in the story is real.

Sometimes a story has vitality, but it needs a photograph to highlight that vitality. Photographs are especially suited to bringing out the action and human interest in a story.

Photo Assignments

Whenever you get a photo assignment, consult with the section editor and the reporter to determine how to make the most of a photograph's functions. In particular, which major point in the story can best be highlighted with a photograph?

You should also get a completed photo assignment form. Make sure the following items are specified on the form:

- story slug (p. 128)
- photographer's, reporter's, and section editor's names
- deadline(s)
- time and date of the shoot
- location of the shoot
- subject or event
- contact person (if any) and phone number
- preference (if any) for vertical or horizontal orientation
- suggestions and instructions

The Shoot

If you're covering an event, be prepared to shoot from various places in various conditions—especially if the event is outdoors. Photographers often have to climb around on things and work in bad weather.

If you're photographing the subject of a formal interview, work closely with the reporter. Decide who will schedule the shoot. Review the details of the assignment before you go. Then get it done in a timely manner; the reporter may need to incorporate details from the photographs into the story.

If the event is important, take backup equipment. For a critical shoot, schedule two photographers.

At the shoot, remember to record the necessary information for the cutline (p. 72). Like reporters, carry a notebook to take down this vital information. Be a stickler for accuracy.

Photo Release

Generally, photojournalists can take photos of people in public places and use them freely without permission. If you take photos of people in their homes or in another nonpublic place, you may want to get a **photo release** from each person.

A photo release is a form that gives the photographer permission to take and use a photo of someone. If you decide to reprint a photo in a publication other than your school paper, you may need a photo release from the parents or guardians of anyone under 18. Check with your adviser.

Camera Operation

Cameras are a part of our culture. We use them to visually record meaningful moments of our lives—including newsworthy events.

You've probably operated a camera, but do you know how it works? Basically, reflected light from a scene enters a small opening in the camera. The light strikes a light-sensitive surface, creating an image of the photographed scene.

In most cameras, the surface is the **film.** The film is a thin piece of plastic coated with silver particles that turn black when exposed to light.

In digital cameras (p. 182) the light-sensitive surface is a solar cell that transforms light into electronic signals, which are recorded on a computer chip. No film is required.

Parts of a Camera

All cameras have the following basic parts:

- **body:** the light-tight box that houses the camera parts
- **lens:** the part of the camera through which the light enters, is sharpened, and is transmitted to the film or solar cell. The focal ring on the lens adjusts the focus of the lens.
- **shutter:** a device that slides back and forth to control the amount of time the film or solar cell is exposed to light
- **shutter-release:** a mechanism to release the shutter
- **aperture:** the lens opening that controls how much light gets through the shutter
- **viewfinder:** a framing device that allows the photographer to see the picture before it's taken

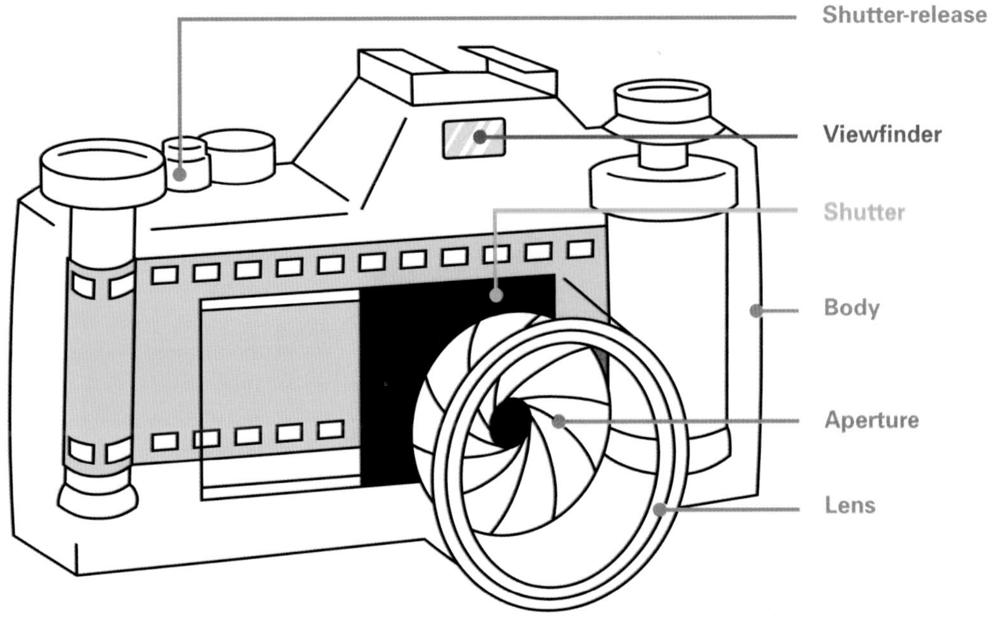

Camera Settings

Other parts of a camera may indicate operational settings for some of the basic parts. These settings include the following:

- **f-stop:** indicates the aperture (lens opening) in numbers. The lower the number, the wider the aperture. With each increase in f-stop, half as much light is let in through the aperture.
- **depth-of-field scale:** indicates the depth of field (p. 185) when the camera is focused on a subject at a particular f-stop
- **shutter speed:** indicates how fast the shutter opens and closes, measured in fractions of a second. The higher (or faster) the shutter speed, the less light is let in through the shutter. With each increase in shutter speed, half as much light is let in through the shutter.

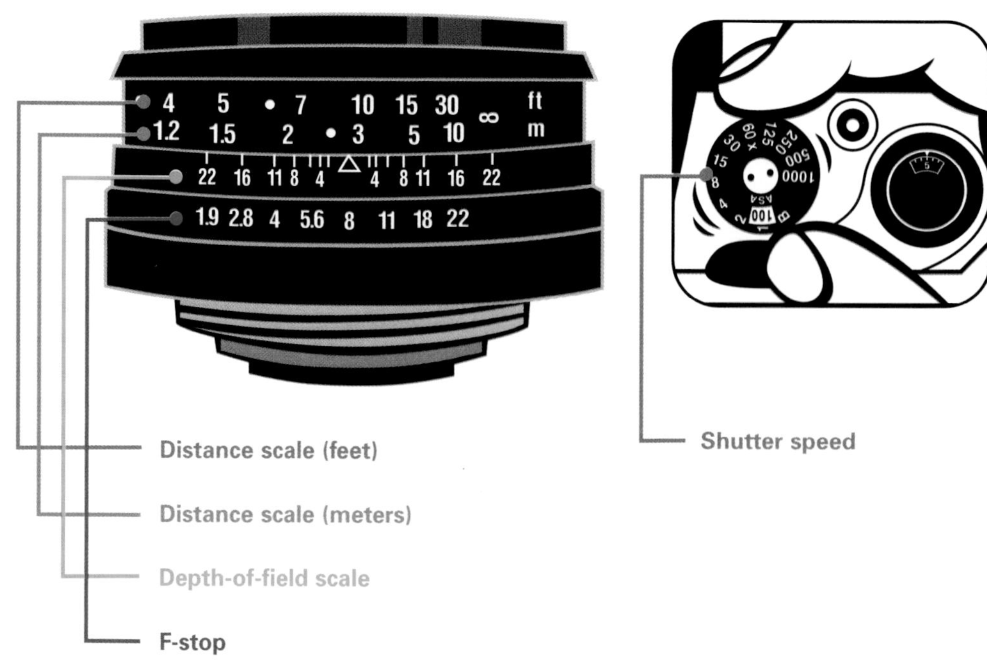

Lenses

A lens is measured by its **focal length** in millimeters. The lower the lens number, the shorter the focal length. The shorter the focal length, the wider the lens. Lower lens number = wider lens.

Lenses fall into three broad categories:

Wide-angle: This type of lens takes in more of the scene than a narrower lens does. But it stretches perspective (the perception of how objects are placed in a scene). It makes the elements in a scene appear farther apart than they are in reality.

Telephoto: This type of lens has a long focal length. It magnifies the elements of a scene, making them appear crowded together and closer to the camera than they actually are.

Zoom: This is a variable-length lens. You can vary the focal length between wide-angle and telephoto focal lengths.

Obviously, some lenses are better suited to certain types of photos than others. This chart will guide you.

Lens Type	Focal Length	Use
Fish-eye	7.5 or 15 mm	Panoramic landscapes
Wide angle	28 or 35 mm	Large-group shots
Normal	50 mm	Candid, everyday shots
Short telephoto	85, 105, 135 mm	Informal portraits
Long telephoto	200 or 300 mm	On-the-spot news (especially sports)
Very long telephoto	400 mm or longer	Wildlife

Types of Cameras

Student journalists may use any of several common camera types. Most of these cameras use 35 mm film, a format that creates a rectangular-shaped photograph.

35 mm SLRs: The 35 mm single-lens-reflex (SLR) camera is the choice of most photojournalists. It has a WYSIWYG (what-you-see-is-what-you-get) viewfinder and interchangeable lenses. Many SLRs include autofocusing and other automatic features. The automatic features usually have a manual override.

35 mm compacts: Most compact cameras are fully automatic. Some have an autofocus feature that enables the lens to work at a variety of distances. Less-expensive models have a fixed focus. Only subjects four feet away and greater will be in focus.

The disadvantage of compact cameras is that they don't allow you to add other lenses. Some models do offer a built-in zoom lens.

Digital cameras: Like 35 mm film cameras, these come in compact or SLR models. A distinct advantage of the digital camera is that it allows you to see your picture immediately after taking it. You can store the image or delete it. Using special software, you then download your selected images from the camera's computer chip into your computer.

Check with your printer about issues related to printing images from digital cameras. And make sure anyone who works with the cameras is trained in the use of the required software.

Exposure

The **exposure** is the amount of light that strikes the film or solar cell in a camera. An overexposed image appears too dark. An underexposed image appears too light.

Four variables influence exposure: the film speed, the light levels of the scene, the f-stop, and the shutter speed.

Film Speed

Films are rated by **film speed,** which reflects their sensitivity to light. The speed is indicated by a number: 100, 200, 400, and so on. The lower the number, the "slower" the film and the less sensitive it is to light. "Faster" film is more light sensitive.

Choose the right film speed for the lighting conditions of your shoot. Shoots at night and in low light require high-speed (faster) film. Bright or outdoor shoots require low-speed (slower) film.

Film speed is also directly related to image quality. Faster film produces a grainier, less sharp image than slower film. Because enlarging an image also causes it to become grainier and less sharp, avoid enlarging images shot with high-speed film.

Light Levels

Automatic cameras adjust to light levels for you by means of a built-in light-metering system. It averages the light in a scene and sets an appropriate f-stop and shutter speed for the film speed.

Adjustable cameras may have a light-metering device in the viewfinder. It indicates whether you need more or less light based on the light levels, film speed, f-stop, and shutter speed.

Professionals often use hand-held light meters. This allows them to take readings from various parts of a scene. Such readings are often more accurate than those of an automatic light meter.

The F-Stop/Shutter-Speed Relationship

On adjustable cameras, you can determine the f-stop and shutter-speed settings. This gives you flexibility not only for getting a correct exposure, but for focusing (p. 185).

If you need more light, use a lower f-stop (wider aperture) to allow *more* light in. Or decrease the shutter speed to allow more *time* to let in light. If you need less light, do the opposite.

Keep this relationship in mind: Lower f-stops (wider apertures) may require faster shutter speeds. Higher f-stops (narrower apertures) may require slower shutter speeds.

This may illustrate the relationship more clearly. Any of the combinations shown here would admit exactly the same amount of light to the film.

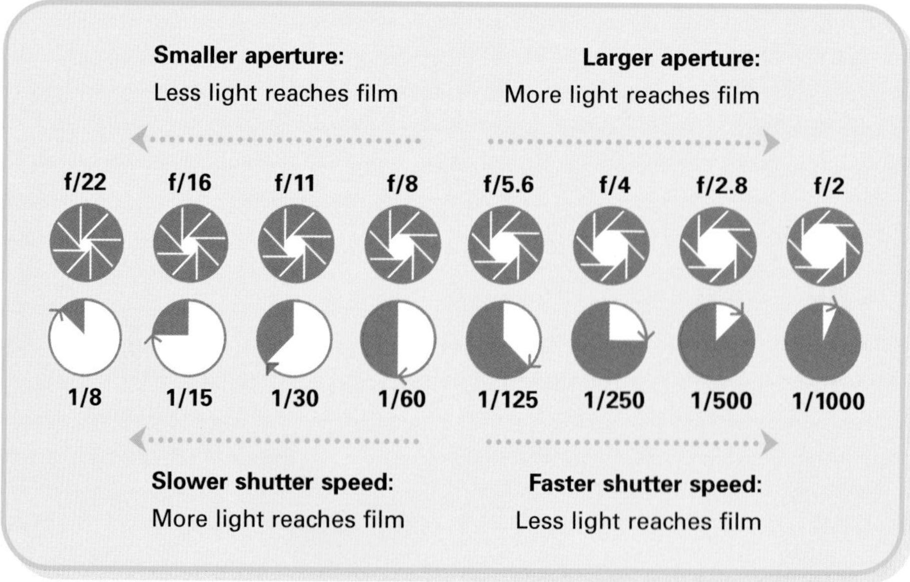

Focus

"Who's that fuzzy person in the background?" That's a question you don't want to hear. With an adjustable camera—and a little practice and patience—you can control what's in focus in your photograph. Most 35 mm automatic cameras adjust to get everything in focus (p. 182).

Depth of Field

The **depth of field** is the area of sharp focus in your picture. Usually this is the area that's in focus behind and in front of the subject. The correct depth of field can make or break a photo.

Some cameras have a depth-of-field preview mode. If your camera doesn't have this feature, use the depth-of-field scale on the focus ring of the lens to determine your depth of field for any particular f-stop.

First twist the focal ring on your lens to focus on your subject. Then find the numbers on either side of the depth-of-field scale that match the f-stop you've set. These numbers express the depth of field as a range. For example, if your focal point is about 10 feet, and your f-stop is f/8, the depth-of-field scale will show you that everything between about 7 feet and 15 feet will be in focus (see the diagram on page 180).

If you want to increase your depth of field, you can do one of three things (the first is the most common):

- Use a higher f-stop (narrower aperture).
- Use a lens with a shorter focal length (wider lens).
- Increase the distance between you and your subject.

Press Time

W. Eugene Smith was one of America's most highly regarded photojournalists. He's credited with pioneering the photo essay. During World War II he was a staff photographer for *Life* magazine. Smith captured many dramatic images from the fighting in the South Pacific. In 1945 he was seriously wounded at Okinawa. After recovering from his injuries, he returned to work at *Life* until 1954. He spent the next 23 years as a freelance photographer.

Photographing Moving Subjects

When you photograph relatively static (nonmoving) subjects, your shutter speed is not as important as other variables. Concentrate on depth of field and then choose a shutter speed to give you a correct exposure (p. 183). When you photograph moving subjects, however, your shutter speed becomes especially important.

You can freeze most moving subjects by using a shutter speed of 1/1000. If your subject is moving head-on or diagonally, you can freeze it at a slower shutter speed than if it's moving horizontally across your field of vision.

To freeze a moving object and blur the background, **pan** your camera with the subject. When you pan, you follow the subject by moving the camera at the same pace and direction as the subject. This creates a photograph in which the subject is in focus but the background is blurred. It takes practice, but the effect is worth it.

Intentionally blurred subjects can be striking too. You might, for example, use a slow shutter speed to blur the swirl of a dancer's skirt or the rush of shoppers in a mall.

Keeping the Camera Steady

Even the smallest movement (by you or the subject) can throw a picture out of focus. You can't always control your subject, but you can learn to keep the camera steady. Here's how:

1. Stand with your legs slightly apart and your back straight.
2. Grip the camera with your right hand, resting your index finger on the shutter release. Cup your left hand under the lens so you can focus it easily and support it at the same time. Keep your arms close in to your body.
3. Inhale. Exhale. Slowly squeeze the shutter release.

If you're using a long lens, use a crouching posture with your right knee on the ground. Rest your left elbow on the other knee to support the long lens. Another option is to stretch out on the ground and use your elbows to support the lens.

For slow shutter speeds, you may want to use a **tripod.** A tripod is a three-legged device on which you can mount a camera. This keeps the camera still while you release the shutter. You can also lean against a wall or tree, or sit cross-legged on the ground, to steady the camera for slow shutter speeds.

Taking the Photograph

Now that you understand the camera and how it works, you're ready to take a photograph that's correctly exposed and focused the way you want it.

TIPS Taking the Photograph

- To help ensure correct exposure, try **bracketing.** To bracket, shoot one picture at what you think is the correct exposure. Then shoot two more of the same picture, one slightly overexposed and one slightly underexposed. One of the three is likely to be correct.
- Keep a record of your shots. In a notebook, list the frame number (the number of the picture, usually shown in a viewing window on your camera), your subject, and your exposure settings. Indicate the f-stop and shutter speed this way: f/2.8 @ 1/250. Compare your data to your finished photographs.
- If you have to set the film speed manually on your camera, do it immediately after inserting the film.
- If you're shooting under a variety of lighting conditions, use a faster film. It's more flexible.
- Finding and processing color film is often less expensive than for black and white film. Even if you print in black and white, you can transform a color print to black and white on the computer or in the halftone conversion (p. 162).
- To minimize problems caused by shaking the camera, use a shutter speed that closely matches the focal length of your lens: *at least* 1/60 for a 50 mm lens, 1/250 for a 200 mm lens, and so on.

Camera Maintenance

Keeping your camera clean and dry is critical to its effective operation. Follow these guidelines for camera maintenance:

- Keep cameras out of direct sunlight.
- Store cameras and film in a cool, dry, dust-free cabinet.
- When you clean your lenses, use *only* lens-cleaning tissues and solutions designed for that purpose. Other glass cleaners will strip the protective coating from your lenses.
- Use a lens brush with a built-in blower to remove small specks of dust on your lens, viewfinder, and the interior mirrors.
- Protect your lens with a lens cap when your camera isn't in use.
- If your camera will be sitting for a while unused, remove any batteries to avoid corrosion.
- Never leave your camera sitting around with the shutter cocked. It puts tension on the springs and shutter mechanism.
- Never touch the shutter curtain inside the camera. It can become distorted, causing problems with shutter-speed accuracy.
- If your camera stops working, have it repaired professionally.

Press Time

Soon after the Japanese bombing of Pearl Harbor in 1941, the U.S. government ordered the relocation of Japanese-Americans into armed camps in the West. The War Relocation Authority hired photojournalist Dorothea Lange to photograph the camps. Lange was deeply disturbed by the racial and civil rights issues raised by the Japanese internment. Her photographs are evidence of human courage amid the indignities and injustices of the incarceration. Many of Lange's photographs were censored by the government.

Lighting

"I have seized the light, I have arrested its flight."

—Louis-Jacques-Mandé Daguerre, inventor of the daguerreotype, the first type of photograph

Lighting is the most important factor in the artistic aspect of your photographs. The light that falls on your subject affects its detail, texture, color, and dimension (whether it appears flat or three-dimensional). These visual qualities combine with the subject and action of the photograph to create a mood.

The mood of your photos may not matter much for small photos, but it can have a major impact on large photos used as a dominant element on a page or in a photo essay (p. 71).

You can learn to seize light by understanding it. In time, you can learn to arrest its flight and create dramatic, effective photographs.

Qualities of Light

Light can be hard or soft, creating harsh or soothing effects. Hard, harsh light usually comes from a single, bright light source, such as the sun or a flash. Soft, soothing light is diffused, or scattered, light. This is the kind of light you get from a shaded overhead light and light outdoors in the shade. It's bright enough to capture details that would be lost in the shadows of harsh light. This makes it perfect for portraits.

Light can also be warm or cool in tone. It takes on the colors of the surfaces off which it bounces. Pictures take on a warm tone when the subject is surrounded by objects with warm (reddish and yellowish) tones. Likewise, when your subject is surrounded by objects with cool (bluish or greenish) tones, your picture will "feel" cool.

For outdoor photographs, the time of day is also instrumental in the quality of light. Early or late in the day, the sun is warm and soft. Midday sun is cold and harsh. Cloud cover can soften light.

Filters

A **filter** is a plastic or glass device attached to the lens of your camera. Filters are available in either the round format, which screws onto the front of your lens or the square format, which fits into a holder. The holder attaches to your lens with a special adapter ring.

Various types of filters are designed to help correct faults, enhance lighting, add creative effects, or control contrast. An ultraviolet filter that reduces atmospheric haze is useful. A polarizing filter is essential. It deepens a sky's blueness and reduces glare.

Front lighting

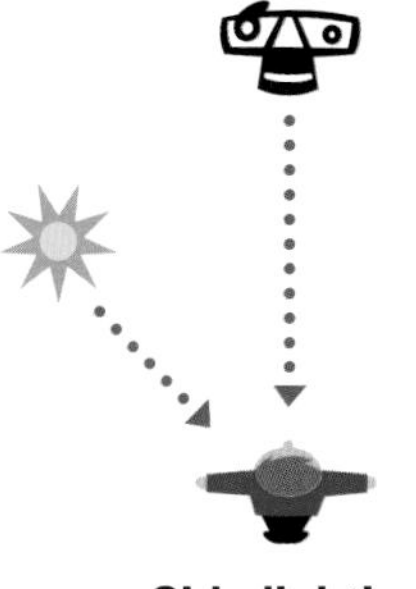
Side lighting

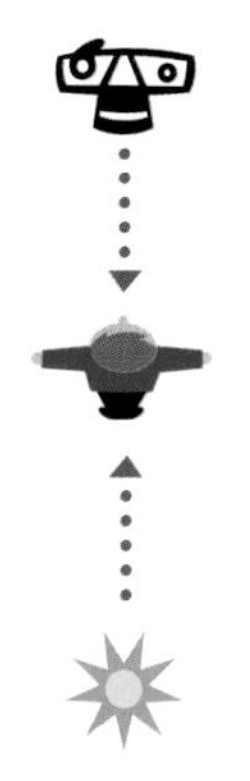
Back lighting

Light Direction

The direction in which the light strikes your subject can dramatically affect the quality of your photograph. These are the basic choices for directional lighting:

Front lighting: Place the light source directly behind you so your subject is evenly lit from the front. This creates a flat picture since the shadows fall behind the subject and may cause a subject to squint. It can, however, work well for outdoor shots taken early or late in the day when subject is bathed in a golden light.

Side lighting: Place the light source to one side of the camera. The light and shadows rake across the scene, highlighting forms and creating depth. This works well for portraits, although you may need to use a **reflector** to fill in details on the shadowed side. A reflector reflects light from the light source back onto the subject. A large piece of white posterboard set on a chair does the trick.

Side lighting is not as effective for photographing buildings, landscapes, and groups of people because parts of the scene may be lost in shadow.

Back lighting: Place the light source behind the subject. With an automatic exposure, you'll end up with silhouettes—not great for pictures of people, but sometimes striking for landscapes. If you adjust your exposure for your subject only, your background will essentially disappear.

Beware of **flare** when you shoot into the sun. Flare is the appearance of a series of bright white circles in your image. To help prevent flare, use a **lens hood,** a device that shields the lens from direct sun.

Using a Flash

Many cameras include a built-in, automatic flash. That's fine for most short-distance work. But for sports photography, large-group pictures, and other situations in which you need to light a scene from a distance of more than eight feet, you need a separate flash unit. It may be handheld or mounted on the camera.

A flash helps fill in shadows and give definition to a picture. But it can also cause a picture to look harsh. Using a separate flash unit, you can bounce the flash off walls to soften the light. Bounce the flash off a white or neutral surface or the flash will take on a color cast. Make sure you know whether your flash unit automatically compensates for loss of light due to reflection and absorption. If it doesn't, you'll need to adjust your exposure (p. 183).

Glass Glare

Don't use a flash when photographing something directly in front of a mirror or other glass surface. If you do, the light will reflect into the lens, causing a glare in your photograph. Instead, shoot at a 45-degree angle when the subject is in front of glass.

Red Eye

When the flash is close to the lens and on nearly the same plane as the subject's pupils, it can cause the subject's eyes to appear red in the photograph. This doesn't matter if you print in black and white, but it can ruin a photo that you need to print in color.

Some cameras have a feature that flashes a light before the actual flash. This helps prevent "red eye," but may cause subjects to look away just before your picture is taken. To be safe, use a separate flash unit, positioned on a plane above the subject's eyes..

Composition

What sets photographers apart from those who shoot snapshots is an eye for composition.

Photojournalism is often spontaneous. You see something newsworthy, and you shoot. Yet even the most experienced photojournalists have learned that you have to stop long enough to consider **composition.** Composition is the arrangement of the elements in the photograph.

You may compose a photograph that is visually appealing, but as a photojournalist you must concentrate primarily on the communication function of your image (p. 175). Your photograph should tell a clear and simple story. For it to do this, you need to absorb and apply certain rules of composition.

The Rule of Thirds

Many cameras include a circle in the center of the viewfinder that serves as a focusing tool. It's *not* a target for positioning subjects! Subjects placed smack in the middle of a frame create a static, boring photograph. By following the **rule of thirds,** you can avoid this humdrum visual arrangement.

As you look through your viewfinder, divide the frame by thirds horizontally and vertically to form a grid—like a tic-tac-toe board. Place your main subject on one of the intersecting points of the grid. Other subjects may be placed diagonally opposite to create dynamic tension. Horizon lines should be along the top or bottom line of the grid.

Filling the Frame

Fill your frame with the image. This means you should get up close whenever you can. You don't have to include all of a subject in a picture—just the most interesting feature. For pictures of people, this is usually the face.

Background and Foreground

No matter how close you get, watch the background. It may add context to a photo. In that case, play it up. But if it's distracting, move yourself or your subject to minimize the distraction. Another option is to adjust your depth of field (p. 185) so the background is out of focus.

Pay attention to the foreground too. Remove distracting objects if possible. Use the foreground to your advantage when you can. An overhanging branch or another object in the corner can create a subtle framing device. It also adds depth.

Angles and Viewpoints

Always take more than one photograph of each scene. This gives you options. One shot may serve better than another.

Take the same photo from different angles—from above, below, to the side, and so on. Be mindful of how angles affect the overall image. Photos taken from above make a subject appear smaller. Photos taken from below make a subject appear larger.

Move around the scene and shoot from different viewpoints. Take a photo from the bleachers to show the crowd's viewpoint. Take a photo from behind the speaker at the podium to capture the speaker's perspective.

Posed Group Shots

Avoid photographing large groups (more than 10 people), especially in small photos. Determine the news makers in the group and concentrate on them.

Keep small groups close together to avoid space gaps between heads. Or shoot from a side angle to minimize the problem. Check your depth of field (p. 185) to make sure everyone is in focus.

Don't be afraid to rearrange your subjects in these posed shots. Try different settings and seating arrangements. Encourage your subjects to relax. Aim for informality.

Leading Lines

People can't resist following lines wherever they go. Use lines within your composition to lead viewers to important subjects in the scene. Lines may be formed by walls, telephone lines, roads, fences, and even shadows.

Horizontal lines are restful, whereas vertical lines imply action. Diagonal lines are the most exciting and powerful.

Action

Take candid photos of people engaged in activity. They communicate more and are more interesting visually.

Look for peak interest in the action, especially in sports photography. But avoid overusing photographic clichés, such as the basketball lay-up shot. Capture unique moments—on and off the playing field: an excited fan tossing a bag of popcorn into the air or a coach's proud face during award ceremonies.

Processing and Editing

"I know few things in the range of science more surprising than the gradual appearance of the picture on the blank sheet."

—William Henry Fox Talbot, inventor of the negative-positive process

Taking the photograph is only the first step in photography. Unless you're using a digital camera (p. 182), the film must first be processed. **Film processing** involves the developing and printing of photographs from film.

Some schools have a **darkroom,** which is a dark room where photographs can be processed without interference from natural light. Other schools send their film out to be processed.

After processing, the images are edited. Just as copy is edited to tell the story better, so a photograph is edited to tell its story better.

Developing and Printing

If you plan to become a photojournalist, you'll probably end up working with digital images. But it's a good idea to learn how photographs are traditionally developed and printed. This is an overview of the process:

1. The rolls of film are chemically processed (developed) in a darkroom. Dark areas of the film become transparent areas, and light areas become opaque. (The dark areas are where light struck the film.) The resulting frames of processed film are called **negatives** because they show the reverse of the light and dark areas that will appear in the printed photograph.
2. The roll of negatives is cut into strips and hung to dry.
3. In the darkroom, a negative is placed in an **enlarger,** which is turned on. An enlarger is a machine that shines light through the negative, magnifying and projecting the image onto a baseboard below, where the image is focused.

Press Time

Cameras of the mid-1800s used glass or metal plates coated with various chemicals to produce the final image. Because of the complexity of these systems, photography was left mainly to a few skilled professionals. George Eastman changed all that in 1888, when he unveiled the Kodak camera. The Kodak came preloaded with 100 exposures. Once all the film was exposed, the photographer returned the entire camera to the Kodak company. It processed the film and reloaded the camera. The Kodak motto was "You push the button; we do the rest."

4. When the desired image is created, the enlarger light is turned off. Photographic paper (paper treated with light-sensitive chemicals) is placed on the enlarger baseboard.
5. The enlarger is turned on to expose the paper. The amount of light and exposure time is controlled. Light shining through the negative creates an invisible positive image on the paper.
6. The paper is developed in a series of chemical and water baths. The process makes the invisible image visible.
7. The resulting print is dried.

Photoediting

If you process your own photos, you can make some edits in the darkroom. If you have your photos processed in a lab, you'll be working with prints.

Cropping

The process of selecting the best part of the photo to print is called **cropping.** Creative cropping can turn an ordinary photo into an extraordinary one.

In darkroom cropping, you expose only the parts of the image you want to print. To crop prints, either scan them and crop them in the computer or mark them for your printer to crop.

To mark photos for cropping, arrange two L-shaped pieces of cardboard over your image until you've selected the area you want. Then make crop marks on the borders of the photo.

Keep these cropping guidelines in mind:

- Maintain the rule of thirds (p. 195).
- Don't crop too close to the top of a person's head.
- Don't crop at the joints (ankles, knees, waist, wrists).
- Leave more space in front of than behind a person.

- Crop out distracting background objects.
- Leave space in front of moving objects (cars, runners, balls, and so on).

Sizing

You may need to enlarge or reduce a photo to make it fit into a certain space on the page. This is called **sizing.**

Of course, you can do some sizing in the darkroom. And prints can be scanned and sized in the computer. If you have your printer do your sizing, however, you'll need to figure the percentage of enlargement or reduction required.

You can use an inexpensive tool called a proportion wheel to do this. You set the measurements of the current image and the required measurements, and the wheel tells you the percentage of enlargement or reduction required.

Editing photos is easy to do with computer software. Not only does the software permit you to crop and size images but it enables you to alter their content. This may seem to enhance the effect, but it may also be inappropriate and illegal. If you alter a photo for a special effect, it should be obvious to the viewer and should be done for a reason.

News photos should not be altered in any way that distorts the truth. Never delete a person from a photo or change a person's appearance. You may, however, correct technical flaws and make adjustments to enhance a photo's contrast or color.

EXplore / EXpand / EXpress

1 **Explore Your World** Look at two or three photographs in your school or local newspaper. Read the cutlines that go with the photos. In what ways are the photos newsworthy? How do they seem to fulfill the various functions of newspaper photos? How does the quality of light affect the photos? What is the light direction in each of the photos? Which parts of the photo are in focus? Notice their composition. Do they follow the rules for good composition?

2 **Expand Your Skills** If you've operated a camera before, use one now to take several photographs. Bracket your shots and keep a record of your exposures (p. 188). Have your photographs processed and compare them to your photo record. Did they come out as you expected?

If you've never operated a camera, take time to study the parts of a camera that belongs to the newspaper staff. Read the manual to learn more about that model. Working with a photographer on staff, experiment with a few shots. Keep a record of your exposures. Get the pictures processed and review them with the photographer.

3 **Express Yourself** In your Journalist's Notebook, describe what you think would be the ideal photo assignment. Tell how you would plan for it. Then imagine how it would take place. Describe the qualities of light at the scene, the lighting approaches you would take, and the composition of several shots.

Business and Advertising

Budgeting

An old joke asks, "What's black and white and red all over?" The answer? Newspapers.

One place you don't want your newspaper to be "red" is on your financial records. Traditionally, record books showed gains in black ink and losses in red ink.

Newspapers, like all businesses, operate on a budget. A budget is a set amount of money available for a particular purpose. It's also a plan for coordinating income and expenses—money coming in and going out.

When your income is greater than your expenses, you're making a profit. When your expenses are greater than your income, you're losing money. When your income and expenses are nearly the same, your budget is balanced.

Your goal is to plan for profits but to maintain a balanced budget. To do this, you need to know your newspaper's income and expenses. You also need to keep accurate, up-to-date records.

Income

Income sources for school newspapers include the following:

Advertising: Sale of advertising space is a primary source of income for many school papers, as it is for the professional press.

Subscriptions: A **subscription** is an arrangement in which a reader pays in advance to receive a publication on a regular basis for a certain period of time. Subscribers may be drawn from the school community and the local community.

School subsidies: School subsidies—funds from the school district—may support all or part of a newspaper budget.

Direct sales: Each issue is sold directly to individual students.

Contributors: Individuals and businesses may donate a minimum dollar amount to be designated a contributor. Contributors are listed in the newspaper.

Grants: Many local foundations and associations award funds based on grant applications or proposals from deserving groups.

Civic clubs: School or community civic clubs sometimes support school newspapers in exchange for a feature article on the club.

Parent-teacher organizations: These organizations make it their business to support school activities, often with an annual donation.

Printer: Printers are sometimes willing to donate a portion of printing costs in exchange for a free ad.

Fund-raisers: Bake sales, car washes, and candy sales are typical fund-raisers. Some schools limit the number of fund-raisers.

Staff-parent garage sales: These can be fun as well as profitable.

Vending boxes: Some city newspapers will donate used sidewalk newspaper vending boxes, which can be repainted and placed at stores in the school neighborhood. You might not sell a lot, but it's a great place to put those press overruns.

Expenses

Smart business managers are able to estimate expenses accurately. They learn to do this by studying budget statements from previous years. You'll find that most expenses for school newspapers fall into three broad categories:

Production costs: This is the money it takes to gather the news, assemble the paper, and print or photocopy it. These costs vary from issue to issue, depending on factors such as **press run** (number of copies printed), number of pages, and use of color. Production expenses include office supplies, computer and laser printer supplies, photography supplies, printing (including any halftone conversions), and newsroom expenses (including photocopying, phone bills, and tickets for performances to be reviewed).

Distribution costs: These are all expenses necessary to get your paper into your readers' hands. Such costs may be small or large, depending on your distribution methods (p. 220). Essentially, they include postage, envelopes, and mailing labels.

Miscellaneous costs: These include expenses for subscriptions to news magazines and newspapers, fees for press associations, and any big-ticket items, such as equipment upgrades. (Plan for upgrades at least a year in advance.)

Record Keeping

You can't run a successful business unless you document all financial transactions. Record your transactions on account ledgers, or record-keeping forms.

Use a computer spreadsheet or accounting program to keep your accounts electronically. Or record accounts on paper and create a paper-filing system. Even if you do your accounting electronically, it's a good idea to keep all paper receipts and purchase-orders on file. Keep at least two years of records on file.

You may want to first check with the school bookkeeper before establishing your record-keeping system. The school may have special requirements for keeping school financial records.

Daily Account Ledger

Devote one ledger to recording daily transactions. As the term implies, record these *daily*.

Include a column for each of the following:

- date (the date you recorded the transaction)
- description (where the money came from or went)
- income (by dollar amount)
- expense (by dollar amount)
- balance (by dollar amount)

Record one transaction per line—an income or an expense. At the end of the line, figure the current balance: If it's income, add the amount to the previous balance. If it's an expense, do the same, but subtract the amount.

Use a calculator to compute finances. One error can be a critical one. Always double-check your calculations. If you use a computer program for your daily accounts, it will perform calculator functions for you, but you should double-check your entries.

Running Accounts

In addition to your daily ledger, keep permanent, running accounts. At the end of each month, transfer the information from your daily ledger into these running accounts:

Accounts receivable: On this ledger, record income owed—money you still need to collect. Include who owes, what the amount is owed for, the amount owed, the date billed, the amount billed, the date received, and the amount received.

Accounts payable: On this ledger record expenses. Indicate from whom you purchased an item, the date of purchase, the date billed, the amount spent, a description of the purchase, the date paid, and the amount paid.

Individual accounts: Set up individual ledgers for each advertiser (p. 214). At the top of the form, note the advertiser, contact person and title, address, phone and fax numbers, and e-mail address. Indicate the date of purchase, the ad size, the date of the issue in which it ran, the date billed, the amount billed, the amount received, and the balance due (amount owed).

Managing Your Budget

Use your records to manage your budget. At the end of each month, total income and expenses for the month and year. Rebill those who haven't paid. Then review accounts with your adviser. You may need to revise plans for upcoming issues according to your current budget.

Advertising

"Advertising says to people, 'Here's what we've got. Here's what it will do for you. Here's how to get it.'"

—Leo Burnett, founder of Leo Burnett Company, one of the world's largest advertising agencies

The most obvious way school newspapers can earn income is through ad sales. Advertising can bring in 50 to 100 percent of your income.

Advertising will benefit your newspaper. But it can also benefit your readers, informing them about products and services they want and need.

You have a business relationship with advertisers. When they buy an ad, they're not doing you a favor or making a donation. Advertisers are your clients. Treat them with respect. Learn about advertising. Create successful ads. Each ad will pay off in future sales.

The Ad-Sales Process

This is a rough overview of steps in the ad-sales process:

1. The business manager meets with the editor-in-chief and design editor to determine the needs for ads.
2. The business manager computes advertising needs and makes assignments for ad sales (p. 212).
3. The ad staff contacts and meets with assigned clients.
4. Ad sales and placement are recorded on a run sheet (p. 212).
5. The ad staff writes ad copy (p. 165), if necessary, and prepares thumbnails (p. 144) of ads.
6. The ad staff, with the assistance of the design staff, lays out the ads (p. 163).
7. The copy editor edits the ads. Section editors may edit ads in their sections. All corrections are input and proofread.
8. The business manager approves proofs of the ads.
9. The ad staff sends proofs to clients for approval.
10. Any changes made by clients are incorporated, copyedited, and proofread.
11. The business manager and clients approve final proofs.
12. The business manager bills the clients.
13. The circulation manager sends the issue to each advertiser.
14. The business manager saves a copy of each advertisement and files it with the client's contract (p. 214).

Ad Rates

Advertisers pay for space. In general, the more space, the greater the expense. Display ads (p. 163) are sold by the column inch (p. 164). Classified ads (p. 163) are priced by the word.

You can set ad rates by the column inch or by standard ad sizes (for example, $18.00 for a 4-inch ad). You can also set rates for fractional-page sizes: 1/8, 1/4, 1/2, and full-page. Many papers offer discounts to repeat clients and for large ads and prepaid ads.

The Rate Sheet

At the beginning of each school year, prepare a **rate sheet** that lists ad rates. Distribute it to all advertisers and prospective advertisers.

Your rate sheet should include the following:

- newspaper identification (the name, address, and phone number of your paper)
- rates (including discounts)
- publication dates for the current school year
- advertisement deadlines for each issue
- payment options and procedures
- your business manager's name and phone number
- column widths and sizes of fractional-page ads
- any restrictions on camera-ready ads (p. 166)
- extra charges for spot color (p. 141) or customized graphics

Some schools run personal ads as part of a classified ad section. Personal ads are little notes from one person to another. Your editorial board should decide whether or not to accept this type of ad and whether to accept anonymous personal ads. Personals can often cause embarrassment. They're difficult, if not impossible, to copyedit. They can also lead to potentially difficult legal situations.

Ad Assignments

Before you make assignments, compute the advertising income you need for the issue. Follow these steps:

1. Subtract the total income *other than advertising* projected for the issue from the total expenses projected for the issue.
2. Check the advertiser contracts (p. 214) to see which advertisers have bought ads to run in the issue. Total up the income as well as the column inches for those ads.
3. Subtract the income of the sold ads from your previous total in Step 1. This is the advertising income needed for the issue.
4. Divide the total from Step 3 by the cost of a column inch, according to your rate sheet (p. 211). This is the number of column inches you need to sell.
5. Add the column inches from Step 2 and Step 4. This is how many column inches you need to leave space for in the pages.

The Run Sheet

For each issue create a **run sheet,** a list of ad sales and placement. Direct your staff to fill out the run sheet *immediately* after each sale.

Your run sheet should include the following categories:

- advertiser
- ad size by dimensions (height x width = column inches)
- ad cost
- amount paid (leave space blank if to be billed)
- page assigned (by business manager or designer)

During layout, check the run sheet often. When you reach your advertising goal, direct the ad sales staff to stop selling. If you oversell, you must run the ads instead of the stories.

The Business of Advertising

This part of the newspaper enterprise goes beyond record keeping. It requires you to drum up new business and serve current clients.

Identifying Prospective Advertisers

Suggest and pursue prospective advertisers—new clientss. But don't bombard prospects with your sales force. Only approach a prospective advertiser if you have been assigned the client.

Be choosy. Make sure the business is an appropriate advertiser for a school newspaper. For example, a liquor store wouldn't be a good choice, but a pizza restaurant would be perfect.

Conducting Market Research

One of the best tools of advertising is market research. Students are consumers. Be prepared to sell that idea. Conduct student surveys (p. 83) to determine their buying habits and tastes. Consult resources that specialize in analyzing consumer spending. Prepare a report on your results.

Press Time

Daily newspapers need news that changes daily. A suitable subject matter is the daily fluctuation of the marketplace. In 1719, however, merchants were concerned that the *Boston Gazette* was revealing too much market information. Competition for customers was driving prices downward. After the American Revolution, newspapers increasingly began to focus on economics. In 1820 more than half of the newspapers in seven major U.S. cities had the word *advertiser, commercial,* or *mercantile* in their titles.

Completing Contracts

All financial business transactions require contracts. The contracts you use will constitute an agreement between your business (the school newspaper) and the client (the advertiser).

Your ad contract should specify the following:

- newspaper identification (the name, address, and phone number of your paper)
- client information (the business name, address, phone and fax numbers, and the contact's name and title)
- the signature of the contact, authorizing the contract
- the signature of the newspaper's ad staff representative
- the form of payment
- standardized language of the agreement (what the client agreed to purchase and at what price), with blanks left for specifics
- the specs (specifications) for the ad

Practice filling out an ad contract at school before attempting to fill out your first one with the client. Once you have the signed contract, make a copy and send it to the client. Keep the original on file.

Maintaining Client Files

Each client should have a paper file folder. File these folders in alphabetical order or in categories of products (clothing, restaurants, sporting goods, and so on). Make the folders easy to access.

The file should include the client's running account (p. 208). If you keep accounts electronically, you may include only the most recent monthly budget statement from the account.

Also include **contact records** in the client files. A contact record is a form that documents a contact with a client. Each time you talk to a client, fill one out and file it.

The contact record should include the following:

- the name of the business
- the person you talked to and his or her title
- the contact's phone number
- the date of the visit
- the outcome of the visit
- any requests for follow-up visits or action

The next time you contact this client, first refer to your most recent contact record in the client's file. Use it to brief yourself before the meeting.

Many business managers put **tearsheets** in their client files. A tearsheet is the printed newspaper page on which a client's ad appears. The entire page is torn from the issue. It's common to mail a tearsheet with the advertiser's bill so the advertiser can see the ad on the page.

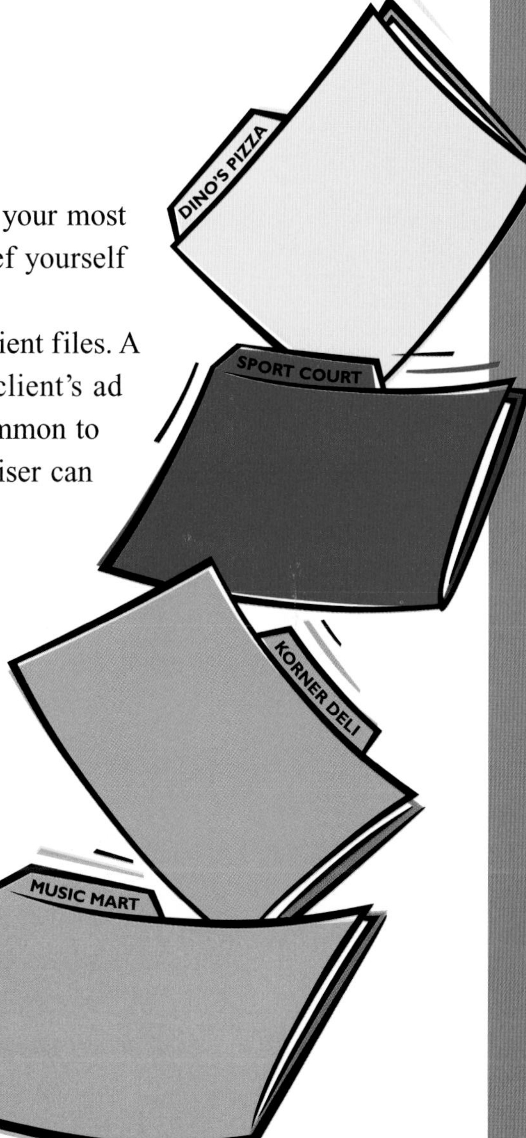

Selling Ads

Selling ads involves more than showing a client a rate sheet and a contract. You have to convince advertisers that they will benefit from placing ads in your paper.

One of the best ways to learn selling techniques is to tag along with an experienced, successful member of the ad-sales staff. Observe. Listen. Then give it a go.

Take special care to prepare. And be persistent. Most ad sales are not made until the fifth visit!

Contacting Your Clients

When you contact your clients, whether in person or on the phone, leave them with a positive impression. You represent your paper.

Follow these guidelines:

- Make your initial contact in person. After you have an established relationship, you and your client may agree to conduct business by phone and fax.
- Dress appropriately for the sales visit. Be neat and courteous.
- Visit your clients regularly to establish a business relationship.
- Each time you visit, fill out a contact record and include it in the client's file.

The Sales Presentation

Every good salesperson prepares a presentation. *Prepares* is the key word. Don't just wing it. Plan and practice.

Typically your sales presentation includes the following:

- **greeting:** a friendly hello followed by an identification of yourself, your paper, and your purpose for the visit (for example, "Hi, I'm Leila Bartlett from the *Tiger Times.* Do you have a few minutes to talk about how advertising in our paper can help your business?")
- **sales pitch:** an explanation of the benefits of buying a product or service (in this case, advertising space in the school paper)
- **close:** a request for a sale (for example, "Now that you've seen what a good deal we offer, can I sign you up for a four-inch ad to run in the next two issues?")
- **wrap-up:** a review of the transaction and plans for the next contact or action

Your sales pitch should explain how your newspaper operates and how the ad will benefit your client by hitting the student market. You may also appeal to how the newspaper benefits the students and community.

The Sales Kit

To give a successful sales presentation, prepare and take along a **sales kit.** Make it professional.

Include the following items:

- rate sheets with sample ad sizes
- two or three issues of the paper
- results of a marketing survey on student spending
- advertising contracts
- your business card (make one if you don't have one)

Press Time

Advertisements prior to the 1800s were basically signs attached to buildings. The signs consisted of symbolic images that identified the product or the name of the business. For example, a boot represented a shoemaker. A hotel named The Sparrow would simply present the image of a sparrow on the sign. Words were seldom used because most people couldn't read. Even later, when public education created more literate consumers, advertisers recognized that simple, symbolic images communicate very efficiently. These signs evolved into company logos, a common part of many ads today.

Public-Service Announcements

Most ads are paid for, but ads from nonprofit organizations are often run for free. A **public-service announcement (PSA)** is an ad that delivers a message from a nonprofit organization.

PSA ads can be useful when you don't sell enough ads to fill the allotted space. Once you run one PSA, however, other organizations may want you to do the same. Your editorial board can decide whether or not to accept PSAs and from which groups.

Selling Ads

- Carry your sales kit wherever you go.
- Familiarize yourself with your client's products and services. You'll be able to make a more convincing sale if you can itemize what students may want to buy.
- Before you meet with a potential advertiser, lay out a sample ad for the business.
- Stress the advantages of print ads. They're inexpensive and can be referred to again and again.
- If you make a sale, let the client know when to expect a proof of the ad and how it will be delivered (in person or by fax).
- After making a sale, take time to explain your paper's billing procedures clearly, using a sample billing form.
- If you don't make a sale, schedule a follow-up visit right away.
- Before you leave, ask for a business card from your client.
- Take time to make the ad as good as it can be. Repeat business is half the battle won.
- Reserve a small space to give a prospective client a "freebee" or to thank a regular client.

Distribution

The papers are here! Now they need to go here and there: onto doorsteps, over the counter, and into the hands of readers.

Professional papers use all sorts of distribution methods, including home delivery, newsstands, newspaper-vending boxes, and mail. Some publish all or part of their papers on the Internet.

School newspapers use some of the same methods. All distribution methods should be approved by the school administration. Remember: The administration is the publisher.

Different methods may be used depending on whether your paper is free or is sold by subscription (p. 205). Some schools offer their paper free to students but charge a subscription fee to other readers to cover mailing costs.

Organizing Distribution

Getting the paper to the readers requires organization. The circulation manager needs to prepare a distribution list and then make assignments. Here's one way to organize distribution.

Readers	**Methods**
Students	Hand deliver in bundles to classrooms at a specified time, such as homeroom period.
School faculty, administrators, and staff	Hand deliver individual copies into office mailboxes and mail a copy to the local superintendent.
School board	Mail one copy to each board member.
School library, lobby, office, and faculty lounge	Hand deliver a bundle to each area.
Other schools in the district	Mail or hand deliver several copies to each school office.
Subscribers	Mail one copy to each subscriber.
Town library and city hall	Hand deliver several copies to each location.
Advertisers and area businesses	Mail one copy to each advertiser and prospective advertiser.
Featured individuals	Hand deliver or mail one copy to each nonschool individual featured in that issue of the newspaper.
Exchange schools and press associations	Mail one copy each to your press association office and other school papers with which you have a newspaper exchange.
Contributors/Patrons	Mail or hand deliver a copy to any individual who donated funds for your newspaper.

Mailing Newspapers

Make sure your mailing list is up-to-date. Check your list with a phone book and zip-code directory. You may want to use a computer a program for mailing lists, which will print out labels.

Self-Mailers

Most school newspapers are mailed out first class in envelopes. You can save money if you design your paper as a self-mailer. If it's lightweight, fold it and seal it with a sticker tab. Leave space on the back page to paste a label. If it's heavy, roll it, wrap it in blank paper, and seal it with tape. Then affix a label.

Bulk Mailing

If you typically mail more than 200 copies of your newspaper, you can use third-class bulk mailing. You pay by the piece, not the ounce (as in first-class mailings). Check with your post office for regulations on labeling and bundling.

Press Time

Newspaper publishers of the 1800s often employed children, called "newsies," to sell their papers on the street corners. Many of these newsies were homeless children who depended on the newspaper trade as their only income. In 1899 publishers William Hearst and Joseph Pulitzer tried to raise the price of their papers. The newsies went on strike, afraid the higher prices would affect sales. Surprisingly, the publishers brought their prices back down. The story was made into a Disney film called *Newsies.*

EXplore / EXpand / EXpress

1 **Explore Your World** Study the advertisements you see in your school and local newspaper. Notice the amount of space the ads take up on the pages. Make a list representing the range of products and services you see advertised. What do the ads tell you about the readers of the paper? Do you see any relationship between what is advertised and where the ad appears in the paper?

2 **Expand Your Skills** Create a list of ideas for prospective advertisers in your area. Next to each notation, explain why you think the business would be a good advertiser for your paper.

When you have a list of 20, review them with your business manager. Get permission to call on at least one potential client on your list. Prepare a sales presentation and kit. Call on the advertiser. Don't forget to fill out a contact record.

If your school paper doesn't use advertisers, do the exercise but perform a role-play of the sales presentation with another classmate portraying the advertiser.

3 **Express Yourself** In your Journalist's Notebook, write a story about how a particular issue of a newspaper comes to your door. Choose one of the distribution methods and follow the newspaper from the printing plant to your hands. You may write the story from the perspective of the newspaper if you like.

Ethics and Responsibilities

Freedom of the Press

"Congress shall make no law respecting an establishment of religion, or prohibiting the free exercise thereof; or abridging the freedom of speech, or of the press, or the right of the people peaceably to assemble, and to petition the Government for a redress of grievances."

—First Amendment to the U.S. Constitution, ratified in 1791

For more than 200 years, the First Amendment has helped protect Americans from limitations on our rights as citizens. It forms the basis for laws that protect freedom of the press and other forms of expression.

But freedom isn't free. You pay for your freedom by being a responsible citizen. In a democracy journalists have a responsibility to keep citizens informed. In this role they serve as a "watchdog" of government, ensuring that authorities act for the common good. The press also has a responsibility to serve as a marketplace of ideas—a forum for sharing facts and opinions on a range of issues.

Understanding freedom of the press will help you fulfill your role as a citizen and a journalist.

Censorship

Censorship is an ever-present threat to freedom of expression. Censorship is the restriction or suppression of material by an authority. Federal laws based on the First Amendment forbid government censorship—except in the public schools.

Hazelwood and *Tinker*

Public school officials have the right to censor school-sponsored student expression according to a 1988 U.S. Supreme Court decision: *Hazelwood School District v. Kuhlmeier.* In this case, a school principal censored articles in the school newspaper that dealt with divorce and teen pregnancy. The *Hazelwood* decision allows such censorship only if it's "reasonably" related to educational concerns.

Prior to *Hazelwood,* student expression was protected as long as it didn't threaten to substantially disrupt the school routine. This was based on a 1969 Supreme Court decision, *Tinker v. Des Moines.* Students in that case had been punished for wearing black arm bands during school to protest the Vietnam War.

Since 1988 some states have passed laws that limit the censorship allowed by *Hazelwood.* Many individual school districts have done the same.

Press Time

In 1798—just seven years after the First Amendment was ratified—Congress passed the Alien and Sedition Acts, primarily in response to the threat of war with France. These Acts made it illegal to print false, scandalous, or malicious words about the government. Numerous journalists were jailed. Even Thomas Jefferson, then the Republican Party leader, admitted that he feared "to write what I think." The Acts expired in 1800. Similar laws were in place around World War I.

Public Forum

A school newspaper has greater press freedom under the *Hazelwood* ruling if it's defined as a **public forum**—a place to freely exchange ideas. With cooperation from your administration you may establish your paper as a public forum. It's good idea to publicly declare this status in your masthead (p. 109).

Prior Review

Your principal may ask to see a story or an entire issue before it's printed. This is called **prior review.** It can lead to censorship. Some states and schools allow prior review; some don't.

Invite your principal to observe your class at work. This can inspire the kind of confidence that will prevent any requests for prior review.

Legal Assistance

If your principal does decide to censor, you and your adviser will have to decide whether it's worth fighting a battle. The following organizations can help you determine whether you have a case and if so, how to handle it:

American Civil Liberties Union
125 Broad St., New York, NY 10036
phone (212) 549-2500; www.aclu.org

The Freedom Forum
1101 Wilson Blvd., Arlington, VA 22209
phone (703) 528-0800; www.freedomforum.org

The Student Press Law Center
1815 N. Fort Myer Dr., Suite 900, Arlington, VA 22209
phone (703) 807-1904; www.splc.org

Unprotected Expression

Some forms of expression are not protected by the First Amendment. Regulations and laws govern this material, which includes the following:

Obscenity: If material is considered offensive by community standards and lacks any serious literary, artistic, political, or scientific value, it's **obscenity.** Nudity, curse words, and "dirty" gestures may be considered obscenity by your community.

Libel: False published material that damages the reputation of a person, business, or product is **libel.** For material to qualify as libel, the libeled subject must be able to be identified and the material must have been published by someone who knew it was false. For example, if you print that your science teacher uses drugs and you know the statement is false, you'll probably be sued by that teacher for libel—and lose. (Libel is more serious than **slander,** which is spoken falsehood, because it's permanent.)

Fighting words: School policies often prohibit so-called **fighting words.** These are expressions that might disrupt school routine—usually insults based on race, ethnicity, religion, or sex. Hate crimes and sexual harassment fall into this category. So does any grafitti that incites students to violent or abusive behavior.

Invasion of privacy: State laws protect private citizens from unwarranted prying by the government and media. A reporter who badgers the survivor of an attempted murder, for example, would likely be violating that person's right to privacy.

Copyright violations: All material is automatically **copyrighted** as soon as it's produced. Copyright is the exclusive legal right to material someone has created. To publish copyrighted material as your own is a violation of copyright law.

Protection Against Libel

Be cautious about any potentially libelous statements. If you're careful and always check your facts, you'll probably be okay. If you're sued for libel, these are your only defenses:

Provable truth: If you can prove that the statement is true, no libel exists. But you've got to have conclusive evidence. And you have to convince a jury that the statement is true.

Privilege: Information presented in legal or official proceedings and reports is **privileged.** This means your account of that information is immune from libel suits—as long as your account is fair and accurate.

Public official/public figure rule: Government officials, including school officials, are **public officials.** Those who purposefully thrust themselves into the news are **public figures.** Sports personalities and movie stars, because of their occupations, are considered public figures.

If you publish false information about a public official or public figure, that person has to prove that you published the false information knowingly and with malice (ill intent).

Public officials and public figures also have a more limited right to privacy than other more private citizens. Public officials must act for the public good and so are under greater scrutiny than other citizens. Public figures choose life in the public eye, so they're expected to accept that people want to know about their private lives.

Fair-comment rule: This rule gives you freedom to express unfavorable opinions about matters of public interest. The comments must clearly be opinions and must be based on stated facts. The fair-comment rule protects reviews (p. 116) from libel.

TIPS Protection Against Libel

- Never shirk fact checking. Check the facts of everything, including attributed information (p. 50). Attributing false information to someone else won't clear you of libel. *You* must confirm that the facts are the facts.
- If your story has the potential to damage someone's reputation, review it with your adviser before you publish it. Make sure you have proof that the potentially libelous statements are true.
- If you make a mistake that's potentially libelous, promptly print a retraction (p. 123). This simple action may cause the courts to excuse you from libelous action.
- Even images can be libelous. Never retouch or alter a photograph in any way that changes its truthfulness or reality. If the original image might be damaging, consider using another image.

Press Time

John Peter Zenger, editor of the *New York Weekly Journal*, was arrested and imprisoned in 1734 for seditious libel—statements that stirred rebellion. Zenger had printed harsh criticisms of the New York colonial governor. At the time, any criticism of the British Crown was libelous—true or not. The eloquent appeal of Zenger's lawyer convinced the jury to return a verdict of "not guilty." The core of the argument was that the statements could not be considered libel unless they were false.

Responsible Journalism

Ethical behavior isn't governed by law. It's governed by you.

In addition to abiding by laws and policies that define the limits of a free press, journalists should follow a code of **ethics.** Ethics are standards for right and wrong behavior. Some ethics are essentially common sense and courtesy—what the general public would consider "appropriate" behavior.

Unethical journalists who cross the lines of appropriate behavior have given the press a bad name. Many people today view the press as rude and ruthless vultures who prey on tragedy and scandal. They accuse journalists of bias and inaccuracy—even outright favoritism and lying.

To earn the trust and respect of the public, you have to be a responsible journalist. You have to report the truth, answer difficult ethical questions, and watch where you step.

Code of Ethics

Your staff should have a written code of ethics—and follow it. You may include it as part of your editorial policy (p. 109).

Include in your code some of the topics addressed in the "Caution" features in this book: "fluffy" content (p. 10), sensationalism (p. 18), off-the-record information (p. 33), investigative reporting (p. 83), manipulating photos (p. 209), and personal ads (p. 211).

Many papers follow the code of ethics written by the Society of Professional Journalists. You may adopt that code or use it as a basis for creating your own. It's organized around four principles:

Seek truth and report it: "Journalists should be honest, fair, and courageous in gathering, reporting, and interpreting information."

Your code should specify guidelines for ensuring accuracy (p. 37) and objectivity (p. 38).

Minimize harm: "Ethical journalists treat sources, subjects, and colleagues as human beings deserving of respect."

Include in your code a warning against bad taste and invasion of privacy (p. 227). And encourage sensitivity, especially when covering emotional or controversial stories.

Act independently: "Journalists should be free of obligation to any interest other than the public's right to know."

Make sure your code states that journalists should not receive gifts or favors from anyone associated with newspaper business. It may seem to influence the newspaper.

Be accountable: "Journalists are accountable to their readers, listeners, viewers, and each other."

In your code stress the importance of serving your readers. Include a commitment to correct mistakes promptly. Vow to expose unethical practices by other journalists.

Being a Responsible Journalist

Being a journalist is a challenge and an adventure. Being a responsible journalist is a challenge and an adventure and a duty.

You can do it. Just keep your head up and your eyes open. Follow your code of ethics and the tips for protection against libel (p. 229). In addition, these tips may help.

TIPS Being a Responsible Journalist

- Make sure the sources of your information are reliable and trustworthy. Be skeptical if the office of the expert you're interviewing is a phone booth on the corner of Main and Pine. And don't use anonymous sources (p. 20).
- Don't ever make up or fake anything—in words or images—even if it seems like a tiny unimportant detail that no one will know or care about. Fabrication of any information is unethical.
- Be sensitive to politically correct (PC) language. It's easy to innocently outrage someone with a bad choice of words. Follow current, nonoffensive usage in reference to race, religion, age, sex, nationality, and physical or mental disability. You may want to include a list of PC terms and usage rules in your stylebook (p. 122).
- Avoid asking sources personal questions. In-depth and investigative reporting may call for such questions, but take care that you don't cross the line into invasion of privacy (p. 227).
- Make sure quotes aren't taken out of context. In other words, include enough of the entire quote to represent fairly what the source said.
- Avoid using any off-the-record information (p. 33) unless you can verify it with at least one other reliable source.

Press Time

One of the most scandalous frauds in journalism history revolved around a Pulitzer Prize winner. Janet Cooke, a young and talented reporter for the *Washington Post,* won the prize on April 13, 1981, for her story on Jimmy, an eight-year-old heroin addict. That day, her editors discovered she had lied about the impressive credentials on her résumé. Later that night, she confessed that Jimmy didn't exist. She made him up based on interviews for the story. The prize was returned and Cooke's journalism career was over.

- If you include a criticism of a person or organization in a story, permit a chance to respond to that criticism in the same story. This is called **right of reply.**
- One community may consider something obscene that another may not. Always consider the standards of your local community. They form the basis of the law against obscene materials.
- When you review a performance, remember the fair-comment rule (p. 228). Stick with commenting on a bad production rather than singling out a bad performer. It's hard to back up opinions about an artistic performance with facts.
- If you have *any* ethical or legal questions about your work, consult with your editor-in-chief and your adviser.

1 **Explore Your World** Review supermarket tabloids, which are known for libelous and unethical stories. How many potentially libelous statements can you find? How do you think these papers get away with this type of behavior? What do you think should be done about it?

2 **Expand Your Skills** Research your state laws concerning students' freedom of expression. Write a few paragraphs that summarize the laws. Then review your own school's policies. Do they give students any further freedom of expression beyond *Hazelwood?* Do they further limit student expression?

3 **Express Yourself** Share your personal views of journalists in your Journalist's Notebook. Do you think they deserve the criticism they get from the public? Why or why not? How have your views about journalists changed since you started learning more about the profession?

Beyond the School Newspaper

Opportunities in Journalism

Your journalism skills can take you places you never imagined—in print, on the air, and on line.

Newspaper journalism skills are almost instantly transferable to every form of news media: magazines, TV, radio, even the Internet. The skills you learn in publishing a school newspaper can also give you a head start in the broader world of communications.

You may want to start by transferring your skills to other forms of school journalism: your school yearbook, literary magazine, Internet publications, or school broadcast station. Or you may want to leap right into the world of professional journalism and explore various journalism careers.

Either way, be prepared to learn. A journalist is constantly challenged with new information and advancing technology.

Professional Newspapers

Every city, and just about every small town, has a newspaper. Working on a professional newspaper gives you the chance to add to the writing and publishing experiences you have. It also gives you the opportunity to polish your skills under the guidance of professional journalists.

Many newspapers would jump at the chance to have an experienced student **correspondent** supplying news from an area school. A newspaper correspondent is a reporter who contributes stories from an area outside the regular beats of the newspaper. If your interests are in the editorial line, you might offer yourself as a regular or periodic columnist (p. 114).

A **stringer** is another position that your local paper may be willing to offer you. Stringers usually work on a freelance basis and send in stories from time to time. Working as a freelancer means that you're not officially on staff. You're paid by the story.

Internships

If you can't get paid work, you may be able to swing an **internship** at a professional newspaper or other local publishing business. Interns are often unpaid. They may run errands for busy staff members, file papers, and answer the phones. They may also have a chance to do some research, writing, or photography.

Internships can be after school, during the summer, or both. It's even possible that your school will give you academic credit for the experience. You may have to propose the internship to the business. Ask your adviser for help in writing a proposal.

School Yearbook

Some school journalism staffs publish the school newspaper *and* the yearbook. Although working on both can be stressful, it's one way to improve your journalism skills—perhaps without even leaving the room. If your school has separate staffs for these publications, you might offer to contribute stories or photos to the yearbook. Just remember: You will have to meet your newspaper deadlines as well as those for the yearbook.

Yearbooks differ in a few distinctive ways from newspapers. First, the reporting isn't timely. That means you'll have more time to get the job done, although you'll still have deadlines hanging over your head.

The second difference is that a yearbook is permanent. Unlike a newspaper, which eventually gets tossed out, a yearbook may stay with its owner forever. You'll savor the satisfaction you get from seeing your stories in hardcover and from knowing that you've contributed to a cherished possession for so many classmates.

Working on a yearbook offers a unique challenge to newspaper staffers. Yearbooks emphasize photography more than a newspaper and are more design intensive, so photographers and designers can show their stuff.

Yearbook copy is spare, but what's there has to sparkle. Reporters will get more than enough practice writing catchy leads and concise copy. They'll be experts at news features (p. 90) before the year is out.

Section editors on yearbooks often supervise entire teams of reporters, photographers, and designers. The editor-in-chief has the challenge of planning coverage for the entire year before the year even begins.

Magazine Publishing

Many schools have **literary magazines.** These magazines publish student fiction, poetry, art, and photography. Some schools publish literary magazines annually, while others manage to publish quarterly (every three months).

Working on your school's literary magazine—or contributing to it—presents you with an opportunity to focus on a range of writing forms. It also introduces you to the practical experiences of magazine publishing.

School literary magazines provide an outlet for your writing and photography at the local level, but you may want to venture into the vast realm of special-interest magazines. Some are interested only in work from adults, but many specialize in writing by and for students. Check your library for writer's-market guides, which tell you exactly what type of material a magazine publishes and how to submit manuscript for consideration.

Press Time

John H. Johnson began his publishing career in 1942. With only $500 to work with he launched his first magazine, *Negro Digest*. In 1945 he began publication of *Ebony* magazine; it was an immediate success. For the next 20 years Johnson's publication would be the only magazine in the United States oriented toward African Americans. At first he had trouble attracting advertisers, so he opened his own mail-order business and advertised its products through his magazines.

Book Publishing

With your writing, editing, and desktop publishing skills, you could be ready to publish your own book. You might even form your own book-publishing company with other classmates. Students have successfully published books independently, sometimes as fund-raisers for school newspapers.

Topics are wide open. You might publish a cookbook featuring recipes from people in your community, a "yellow pages" directory targeted toward students, or a "best-of-our-city" guide.

Before you take on any undertaking as big as publishing a book, do a little market research. Canvass local and Internet bookstores to determine how many other books exist on your chosen topic. If there are dozens, will yours be able to compete? If there are none, is anyone really interested in this type of book?

Most independent publishers have a hard time raising the money for printing, marketing, and distribution of books. If you want to reach a broad, national audience, you'll have to sell your idea to a big publisher. But don't try to go directly to the publisher. Instead, consult a literary agent, who acts as an intermediary for you.

Check the writer's-market books at your library for book publishers and literary agents who might be interested in what you want to write. Be persistent. Even the most successful writers usually fished for years before they got a bite.

Internet Publishing

The Internet has obliterated many boundaries between people. You can now reach anyone who has a computer and a modem. The news media and the business world have latched onto this medium as one of the fastest, cheapest ways to reach a huge population.

Many professional and school newspapers publish all or part of their issues on the Internet, simultaneously with their hard-copy editions. If your school publishes an on-line newspaper or magazine (called a **zine**), you can get involved and learn all about web publishing. If your school doesn't have an on-line publication, perhaps you can launch one.

On-line publications offer a variety of benefits. With inexpensive software, you can turn your computer layouts into web pages almost instantly. And whereas you may only be able to afford to print in black and white, your on-line publications can freely run in color.

In addition to publishing your school newspaper on line, you may want to consider operating your own special-interest web site. It may feature a favorite sport, music star, or hobby. Like many amateur web-site editors, you'll gather, write, edit, design, and maintain your site. You'll become a **webmaster.**

Being a webmaster is perfect for journalists who love technology. And the field is only getting bigger.

Advertising and Public Relations

Advertising and public relations are two more fields in which you can hone your journalism skills. Your skills in writing, designing, photography, and selling advertising are all applicable.

Press Time

Sigmund Freud's nephew, Edward L. Bernays, believed that public relations had more to do with sociology than journalism. Its goal, Bernays said, is to "manipulate public opinion." Bernays wrote the first book on the subject in 1923, and taught the first college course on public relations. He's often cited as the father of the profession. A former reporter, Ivy Ledbetter Lee, could also claim the title. Lee opened a publicity firm in 1904 dedicated to honest and responsible promotion of his clients. Lee is credited with writing the first code of ethics for public relations professionals.

Find out what occupations in these areas are all about by volunteering in an advertising firm or in the public relations department of an area business. Nonprofit organizations, in particular, are often looking for talented volunteers to write copy for brochures and newsletters. Your local nature center, hospital, or youth center may be looking for your services right now.

If you're interested in advertising, get all the experience you can in writing the ad copy on your school paper. This is called **copy writing.** Professional copywriters are creative thinkers as well as good writers. You can make a career out of a talent for catchy slogans and a strong working knowledge of the media.

Public relations frequently involves writing copy for **news releases,** information about an organization provided to the news media by that organization. Public relations professionals also have a keen understanding of the media and must be people oriented. Your experience as a reporter or editor would be a good fit for these requirements.

Broadcast Journalism

Many print journalists make successful crossovers to **broadcast journalism**—radio and TV. It takes extra training to learn to deliver the news on the air instead of on paper.

The best place to get a start is in a school broadcast studio. If you're lucky enough to have a broadcast journalism course or access to a school studio, you're on your way.

If your school doesn't offer courses or have studio facilities, pick up a video camera and practice on your own. In time, you'll become comfortable with microphones and live interviews. You'll learn to be poised before the camera.

Eventually, you may expand your broadcast skills to the local airwaves. Some radio stations have shows produced by teens. And cable TV providers offer public-access channels at which you can gain valuable experience—and exposure.

You may feel more comfortable behind a camera than in front of one. Even in broadcast journalism, there are plenty of jobs for writers and editors, as well as for camera operators—a fairly smooth transition for photojournalists.

EXplore / EXpand / EXpress

1 **Explore Your World** Look around your community for jobs that would make use of journalism skills. Talk to adults you know to get more ideas. What types of tasks do they perform on their jobs that could make use of journalism skills? Make a list of jobs and job tasks. Next to each, list the journalism skills you've learned that would apply.

2 **Expand Your Skills** Choose one of the journalism opportunities described in this chapter and pursue it. You may choose to work with another classmate to start a special-interest magazine or web site. You may decide to join the yearbook staff or get training in broadcast journalism through your school or local broadcast studios. Whatever you do, share your experience with other interested students in a short presentation.

3 **Express Yourself** Write a letter to a prospective employer in the media or communications field. Describe your skills and experience. Explain why you think this employer should create a position or internship for student journalists like yourself. Be sure to spell out how having a student journalist on staff would benefit the employer. Ask for the opportunity to work for the employer. Include this letter in your Journalist's Notebook for future reference and possible use.

Stylebook

Most professional journalists use the Associated Press or the *New York Times* style. Quill and Scroll Society and the Columbia Scholastic Press Association publish stylebooks for student journalists. The stylebook provided here is somewhat simplified compared to these.

I. Abbreviation

A. Try to avoid abbreviations if they're not recognizable to the general public. Spell out the full name at the first mention, immediately followed by the abbreviation in parentheses. After that, use the abbreviation. Avoid starting a sentence with the abbreviation.

> The local chapter of Mothers Against Drunk Driving (MADD) met last week to discuss flyers for their new public-awareness campaign. The MADD flyers present statistics on the number of car accidents involving drunk drivers over the past year.

Some organizations are best known by their abbreviations (PTA, NASA, IRS, FBI). These can be used alone.

B. Abbreviate professional titles only when they come before the name as a title.

Correct

> The well-known internist Dr. Nancy Kostner just arrived.

Incorrect

Nancy Kostner is a Dr. of internal medicine.

C. Months

1. Abbreviate months of the year when used with a specific date.

   The students held an antiwar rally on
   Nov. 17, 1974.

2. Do not abbreviate months when they appear without a specific date.

   The rally took place in November.

3. Do not abbreviate the names of months that contain five letters or fewer (March, April, May, June, July).

Correct

Applications are due April 12.

Incorrect

Applications are due Apr. 12.

D. States

1. Use the zip-code abbreviation for any state mentioned in connection with a city. (Most dictionaries contain a listing of the zip-code abbreviations for all 50 states.)

   Ed Sanchez lives in Los Angeles, CA.

2. Do not abbreviate state names when used alone.

   Ben Hollis is from Rhode Island.

E. Addresses

1. Abbreviate street designations (St., Ave., Blvd., Rd.) when used in a numbered address.

Correct

Take the bus to 1257 Seville Rd.

Incorrect

My aunt lives at 1620 Grand Boulevard.

2. Do not abbreviate street designations when used alone.

Correct

The pharmacy is located on Division Street.

Incorrect

Isn't that shop on Sangre St.?

F. Do not abbreviate units of measurement, except in charts or graphs.

Correct

The quarterback moved the ball upfield to the 50-yard line.

We had 24 inches of snowfall in one day.

Incorrect

Dr. Pennington is 5′2″.

Dr. Pennington is 5 ft. 2 in.

G. Do not abbreviate days of the week, holidays, departments, or job positions.

Correct

teacher	math department
Easter	Monday

Incorrect

Sec.	Treasury Dept.
Xmas	Fri.

H. Avoid the abbreviation *etc.* in news copy. Use *and so on* instead.

II. Capitalization

A. Capitalize all proper nouns. Do not capitalize common nouns.

Correct

The Teraberrys bought their car from Imperial Motors.

Incorrect

The new Biology Teacher is also the Drama Coach.

B. Job Titles

1. Capitalize job titles that come before a proper name.

Correct

The team speaks highly of Coach Lyons.

Incorrect

The discussion was led by Judy O'Casey, a History Professor.

2. Lowercase and spell out job titles when they're not used with a person's name.

The principal spoke at the school board meeting.

C. Capitalize days of the week, months, holidays, and special events.

Correct

The first event of the spring season is the Sunshine Pageant on Friday, March 28.

Incorrect

The shelter provides thanksgiving dinner for the homeless.

D. Capitalize full names of streets, schools, and organizations.

Correct

Flora Edwards attended Gull Lake High School, located on Fifth Avenue.

Incorrect

George Yakima is head of the bedford college beautification society.

E. Do not capitalize seasons, clock abbreviations, or other time designations.

Correct

> In winter the track team practices three times a week at 6 a.m.

Incorrect

> This Fall students will take part in a school cleanup project.

F. Directions

1. Do not capitalize points of the compass in directions.

Correct

> Latimer lives in a small town south of Madison.

Incorrect

> Santa Fe is in Northern New Mexico.

2. Capitalize compass points that indicate specific geographical regions.

> The West Coast had major storms this winter.

3. Capitalize compass points that refer to a particularly well-known section of a city or state.

> Chicago's stockyards are on the South Side.

G. Classes, Grades, Courses, and Degrees

1. Capitalize class designations when they refer to the entire group.

   The Senior Class is organizing a formal dance.

2. Do not capitalize class designations when they refer to individuals.

   Kelly Rosen, junior, won the writing contest.

3. Do not capitalize names of grades.

   He is in the seventh grade.

4. Capitalize names of specific courses, but do not capitalize the names of academic disciplines.

Correct

She prefers science to social studies, so she's taking Introduction to Physics.

Incorrect

Jamal said his biology 101 class is always interesting.

4. Capitalize college degrees when they're abbreviated. Do not capitalize them when they're spelled out.

Correct

B.A. bachelor's degree

Incorrect

b.a. Bachelor's Degree

III. Numbers and Symbols

A. In dates, scores, addresses, ages, time references, and money denominations, use numerals only.

Correct

The score was 2-0.

Gloria asked everyone to contribute $5 for new band uniforms.

Octavio Gutierrez will be 12 years old on Nov. 20.

The track meet will begin at 2 p.m.

Incorrect

The score was two to nothing.

Gloria asked everyone to contribute five dollars for new uniforms.

Octavio will be twelve years old on November twentieth.

The track meet will begin at two p.m.

B. Spell out numbers from one to nine. Use numerals for 10 and above. (Note the exceptions discussed in Part A of this section.) Do not begin a sentence with a numeral.

Correct

The painting class has 10 students.

Students have three chances to pass the test.

Incorrect

25 people showed up for the auditions.

Only 3 roles are available.

C. Spell out approximate numbers.

Nearly six hundred people saw the class play.

D. Use words and numerals for very large numbers.

Correct

The company lost $15 million last year.

Incorrect

She inherited twenty thousand dollars.

E. Spell out fractions for amounts of less than one.

Correct

The auditorium was two-thirds full.

Incorrect

Is the cup 1/2 empty or 1/2 full?

F. For percentages use numerals and spell out the word *percent.*

We only had a 2 percent chance of rain.

G. For temperatures use numerals for everything except zero. Use the word *minus* when referring to temperatures below zero.

The wind-chill factor on Tuesday was minus 5.

Temperatures fell 25 degrees during the course of the day.

IV. Proper Names and Titles

A. For professional titles, use the person's title, first name, and last name in the first mention. After that, use the last name only.

> Dr. Abraham Goldman led the community food drive. Goldman has supervised numerous charitable events.

> Principal Abe Chase won the faculty/staff costume contest. Chase showed up in a Darth Vader costume, complete with a light saber.
>
> Second-place winner was Carrie Fallon, English teacher. Fallon was dressed as Mother Goose.

B. For students, list the first and last name, followed by a comma, the grade, and another comma on the first reference. After that, use the last name only.

Some schools spell out grade references, some use numerals. Use numerals if you want to save space. Be consistent in your use.

> Nina Juarez, 8th grade, was the top scorer. Juarez has led the team in scoring all season.

C. In general, do not use the personal, courtesy titles *Mr., Mrs.,* or *Ms.* unless you must distinguish among people with the same last name.

> When Ms. Jones returned, Mr. Jones was not at home.

At one time *Miss* was commonly used to refer to an unmarried woman; however, the usual practice today is to use *Ms.* instead.

V. Punctuation

In general the standard rules taught in English classes can carry over into newspaper writing.

A. Periods

1. Always use periods in the time designations *a.m.* and *p.m.*
2. Always place periods inside, not outside, quotation marks.

Correct

Juan looked at the sky and muttered, "It looks like rain."

Incorrect

Alicia replied, "Well, then we'll go to the movies".

3. For money amounts of less than one dollar, spell out the word *cents.* Use the dollar sign for money amounts of a dollar or more.

Correct

32 cents

Incorrect

$.32 or 32¢

4. Use a period as a decimal point to separate dollars from cents.

Correct

$14.50

Incorrect

$14.50 dollars

5. When a dollar amount is even, do not use a decimal point and the ciphers (zeros).

Correct

$2

Incorrect

$2.00

B. Commas

1. Use a comma to separate independent clauses.

   Principal Skinner introduced the main speaker, and the listeners immediately rose to their feet.

2. Use a comma to set off a dependent clause that begins a sentence.

   When the game ended, the fans left the bleachers.

3. Use a comma to introduce a direct quotation.

   The clerk said, "Would you like anything else?"

4. Use a comma to separate parts of an address.

   The robbery took place at 251 Rose Ave., Richland, IN.

5. Use a comma to separate figures with four or more digits.

Correct

1,267 50,000

Incorrect

1267 50000

6. Use a comma to separate words in a series, including the last word before the word *and.*

Correct

For dinner they had fish, rice, and salad.

Incorrect

For dinner they had fish, rice and salad.

C. Semicolons

Note: Semicolons are somewhat rare in news stories. Use them sparingly.

1. Use a semicolon to separate clauses of a compound sentence that are connected by words such as *however, otherwise,* or *therefore.*

   He could have passed the exam; however, he refused to study.

2. Use a semicolon to separate independent, but related, clauses that have no conjunction (*and, so, but*).

   The mayor voted for the proposal; the aldermen voted against it.

3. The semicolon always goes outside quotation marks.

   The class had studied "A Child's Christmas in Wales"; they were interested in reading more works by Dylan Thomas.

D. Colons

1. Use a colon to show clock time.

   The theater opens at 7:45 p.m.

2. Do not use a colon for clock times on the hour.

Correct

   The show begins at 8 p.m.

Incorrect

   The show begins at 8:00 p.m.

3. Use a colon before a list of items, especially after expressions such as *the following,* but not after the expression *such as.* Do not use a colon if the list comes immediately after a preposition or verb, including forms of the verb *include.*

Correct

   The fair offered food for everyone's tastes: corn dogs, lemonade, cotton candy, gyros, and veggie tacos.

   Students donated the following items to the Care-for-Kids Camp: tents, sleeping bags, rain gear, cooking pots, and first-aid gear.

Incorrect

She collects: music boxes, bells, chimes, and other items that play "tinkling" music.

He participates in: basketball, Ecology Club, and debate.

Social studies includes: geography, anthropology, and history.

4. Capitalize the first letter following a colon only if it begins a complete sentence.

Correct

The manager made this announcement: The store will stand behind every product it sells.

Incorrect

There was only one thing left at the garage sale: A broken radio.

E. Quotation Marks

1. Use double quotation marks for direct quotes. Use single quotes to set off a quotation within a quotation.

The mayor, responding to the criticism, said, "There is no point in arguing with people who don't understand the issues. My critics say 'Mayor Jackson doesn't listen to our complaints.' Well, folks, here I am. I'm listening."

2. Use quotation marks for the titles of short works such as poems, short stories, TV shows, and songs.

   Robert Frost's "Stopping by Woods on a Snowy Evening" is one of America's best-loved poems.

VI. Formatting Text

A. Italics

1. Italicize titles of newspapers, books, plays, films, magazines, and other full-length works of art.

   The story about Arthur Miller's play *Death of a Salesman* ran on the front page of the *New York Times.*

2. Do not underline or italicize words for emphasis.
3. Italicize words when they are referred to as words or terms.

   He was offended by the term *jock.*

VII. Usage

A. Commonly Confused or Misused Words

accept, except—accept: to agree to; except: to exclude

adapt, adopt—adapt: to adjust or become accustomed; adopt: to accept or take as one's own

affect, effect—affect: to pretend; effect: the result of a cause

all ready, already—all ready: completely prepared; already: "before now" *all together, altogether*—all together: as a group; altogether: completely

a lot, allot—a lot: a large amount; allot: to assign a part or portion

altar, alter—altar: a small raised structure used for religious purposes; alter: to change

can, may—can: is able; may: is allowed or permitted

capital, capitol—capital: city where a center of government is located; capitol: important building within a capital city

complement, compliment—complement: add to in a positive manner; compliment: express respect for or admiration

complementary, complimentary—complementary: serving to complete; complimentary: free

convince, persuade—convince: to satisfy by reason or argument; persuade: to bring about

farther, further—farther: refers to physical distance; further refers to extent or degree

fewer, less—fewer: deals with actual numbers; less: d with a nonspecific quantity

lay, lie—lay: to place (as in "lay the dress on the table to recline (as in "lie down on the bed")

principal, principle—principal: person, place, or is first in importance; principle: a fundamental tru *their, there, they're*—Though the meanings of these words should be well known to you, be careful not to confuse them in your writing.

to, too, two—Though the meanings of these words should be well known to you, be careful not to confuse them in your writing.

B. Politically Correct Terms

Outdated Term	*Current Term*
fireman/firewoman	firefighter
chairman/chairwoman	chairperson, chair
housewife	homemaker
mankind	humankind, humanity
postman, mailman	postal worker, mail carrier
alesman	sales representative, salesperson
esman	representative, spokesperson
man/businesswoman	businessperson
/policewoman	police officer
	waiter, wait staff
	actor

Research Resources

Encyclopedias

Many types of encyclopedias from various publishers are available, some on CD-ROM and by subscription on the Internet. They're published annually. Use the most current edition available.

World Almanacs

Published annually, almanacs contain a wealth of up-to-date factual information on thousands of subjects, such as the most popular movies, world leaders, and sports events results. Almanacs are available from various publishers.

Biographies

Libraries typically have several biographical dictionaries, some of which are available on CD-ROM. *Current Biography: Who's News and Why* (H. W. Wilson) profiles people who are currently prominent in the news. *The Dictionary of American Biography* (Charles Scribner's Sons) and *Webster's Biographical Dictionary* (Mirriam-Webster) offer brief bios of notable people. *The Who's Who books* (Marquis Who's Who) offer biographical information on "somewhat" famous people.

Statistics

Books of statistics available in most libraries include the *Book of Vital World Statistics* (Times Books/Random House) and the *CIA World Factbook,* available in print and on the Internet from the Central Intelligence Agency (CIA). These books, published annually, list statistics about the countries of the world.

Addresses

Telephone directories offer not only phone numbers but addresses. In addition to local directories, some city libraries may have out-of-town directories. For city, county, state, and federal government listings, check the *Government Phone Book USA* (Omnigraphics, Inc.). To contact celebrities, athletes, national broadcast networks, publishers, and more, try the *Kid's Address Book* by Michael Levine (Perigee Books).

Magazines

The most common search tool for periodicals is the *Readers Guide to Periodical Literature* (H. W. Wilson), which provides listings of articles, by subject, that appear in hundreds of magazines. Print volumes and CD-ROM versions are published annually. You can also search for magazine articles using various Internet search services (see Computer Research Resources). Or check out magazine web sites to search for articles in their archives.

Newspapers

All libraries carry local as well as regional newspapers. Most also carry prominent papers such as the *New York Times* and the *Wall Street Journal.* Issues older than one year will probably be on microfiche or archived electronically. Many newspapers have archives on their web sites where you can access articles—for free or for a fee.

Historical Archives

Some libraries are archives for local and regional historical documents, including historical photographs and documents such as maps and government records. School libraries usually have back issues of school yearbooks and newspapers.

Computer Research Resources

Nearly every library offers access to the Internet, which provides information on just about any topic. Infotrac, an Internet-based guide, provides text of recent articles from nearly 200 newspapers and magazines. It includes a built-in search feature. Many libraries have CD-ROM encyclopedias, some with links to the Net. And most libraries have an Internet connection to the catalogs of other libraries, so you can arrange to borrow books that your library may not have.

Glossary

advance story a story that focuses on an event in the near future

alignment refers to any line created as a result of the way page elements are arranged

anecdote a short account of an interesting, powerful, or humorous event

angle the approach a reporter takes to a story

anonymous source an unnamed SOURCE

aperture in a camera, the opening in the LENS that controls how much light gets through the SHUTTER

attribution a phrase that tells the SOURCE of the information given

back lighting in photography, lighting in which the light source is behind the subject

balance the design principle that reflects the stable, yet dynamic distribution of elements in a design

banner a bold HEADLINE that runs the entire width of the page

base alignment the alignment of the BASELINE of COLUMNS of type next to each other

baseline the bottom of a line of type

beat an area or SOURCE of news that's regularly covered by a specific reporter

benefit heads in a DISPLAY AD, the HEADLINE and SUBHEAD that grab the reader's attention and explain the benefit of responding to the ad

bleed the running of a photo or other GRAPHIC through the EXTERNAL MARGIN and off a page

blind lead a LEAD that begins with an interesting fact and leads the reader into the following paragraphs to get the specifics

body in a camera, a light-tight box that houses the camera parts

body type type used for COLUMNS of copy

bracketing a method by which a photographer shoots one picture at the perceived correct EXPOSURE, then overexposes one picture and underexposes another. The basic idea is that one of the three exposures will likely be correct.

broadcast journalism NEWS delivered over the radio or TV

broadsheet a newspaper FORMAT that measures approximately 14 by 21 inches

bullet a centered dot that calls attention to a line of copy or sets off items in a list

byline a credit that tells who wrote a story

callout a short bit of COPY that labels or explains an element in a GRAPHIC

camera-ready a LAYOUT ready to be placed and printed just the way it is

censorship the restriction or suppression of material by an authority

centered alignment ALIGNMENT that provides no line at the left or right margin. Each line is centered within the full COLUMN width.

centerspread or **double-truck** a spread in the center of a newspaper, printed as one sheet of paper

character a type letter (such as an *A*) or letterform (such as a comma)

circulation the total number of people and businesses that receive a newspaper

circulation manager the person who keeps track of a newspaper's SUBSCRIPTIONS and coordinates DISTRIBUTION

classified ad an ad, consisting of a short block of COPY, placed by an individual or business trying to sell a product or service

cliché a trite, overused word or expression

clip art ready-made GRAPHICS available for use free of charge or for a small fee

close in a DISPLAY AD, the COPY that calls readers to action; in a sales presentation, a request for a sale

closed question an INTERVIEW question that allows only one answer, such as *yes* or *no*

cold read a situation in which a proofreader has no HARD COPY of a previous PROOF to compare with the current one and so must just read the current proof

column a BYLINED article that reflects the opinion of a specific writer; vertical section of printed COPY in a newspaper LAYOUT

column inch a measurement for newspaper space. A column inch is one inch high and the width of a newspaper's standard COLUMN.

composition the arrangement of elements in a photograph

conflict an ELEMENT OF NEWS that refers to the tension, surprise, or suspense in a story

consequence an ELEMENT OF NEWS that refers to the effect a story will have on the lives of the readers

consistency the design principle that reflects the application of an identical design to elements that are identical and application of a similar design to elements that are similar

consumer reporting a type of reporting that covers good and bad buys in the marketplace

contact record a form that documents a contact with an advertising client

contrast the design principle that reflects the use of opposites in color, size, and shape to create emphasis and to distinguish one element in a design from another

copy or **text** all words that will be set in print

copy editor the person who checks COPY before it goes into pages to make sure it's factually accurate and conforms to the newspaper's STYLE

copy write to write ad COPY

copyedit to perform the functions of a COPY EDITOR during the final phase in the editing process

copyfit to cut or add words to make COPY fit into an allotted space on a page

copyright the exclusive legal right to material someone has created

correspondent a reporter who contributes NEWS stories from an area outside the regular BEATS of a newspaper

coverage story a story that covers an event that happened in the recent past

crop to select the best part of a photograph to print

cross alignment the horizontal ALIGNMENT of elements across the top of COLUMNS and at the top and bottom of pages

cub reporter a reporter that's new on staff or just beginning in the field

cutline or **caption** information that accompanies a photograph or other GRAPHIC

darkroom in photography, a dark room where photographs can be processed without interference with normal light

dateline a line of COPY that identifies the place where the NEWS occurred

deck one level of a HEADLINE

depth of field in a photograph, the area of sharp focus. Usually this is the area that's in focus behind and in front of the subject.

depth-of-field scale in a camera, a setting that indicates the DEPTH OF FIELD at a particular F-STOP when focused on a subject

desktop publishing the use of a desktop computer to write, edit, design, and prepare pages for publication

direct quote a QUOTE, printed word for word

display ad an eye-catching ad, consisting of COPY and GRAPHICS, placed by a business or organization

display type type used for HEADLINES, BYLINES, CUTLINES, and other special page elements

distribution the delivery of a newspaper into the hands of its readers, achieved by various methods

dominance the design principle that reflects the use of one visual focal point, or DOMINANT ELEMENT, in each design

dominant element a visual focal point that serves as an ENTRY POINT for readers as well as a center of visual interest on a page

downstyle a style of HEADLINE in which only the first word and proper nouns are capitalized

dummy a full-size drawing of a finished page that shows where all page elements will appear

edit to make changes to COPY for the purpose of improving it

editorial a short article that expresses opinions on a topic. By strict definition, an editorial expresses the official opinion of the newspaper and so doesn't have a BYLINE.

editorial board members of a newspaper staff who meet regularly to discuss the newspaper's content and to plan future issues

editorial cartoon a type of EDITORIAL that uses pictures to get a point across. It may illustrate a written editorial or stand alone. Unlike other editorials, it's signed (by the artist).

editorial page the page in a newspaper that's devoted to opinions

editorial policy a statement that explains a particular newspaper's goals, policies, and guidelines

editorialize to include personal opinions in a supposedly objective story

editor-in-chief in a newspaper organization, the next in command behind the PUBLISHER

elements of news the characteristics of a story that make it appeal to readers. These include TIMELINESS, HUMAN INTEREST, PROXIMITY, PROMINENCE, CONSEQUENCE, and CONFLICT.

enlarger a device used to shine light through a NEGATIVE, magnifying the image onto light-sensitive photographic paper, where the image is focused and imprinted

entry point a visual element that draws readers into a story or page

ethics standards for right and wrong behavior

exposure in a camera, the amount of light that strikes the FILM or solar cell

external margin a frame of WHITE SPACE around the LAYOUT marked by the outside edge of at least one GRAPHIC or block of COPY

facing pages two inside pages that face each other but that are not usually printed on the same sheet of paper

fair-comment rule a rule that allows a reporter the freedom to express unfavorable opinions about matters of public interest

family FONTS closely related in style

feature a SOFT-NEWS story

featurize to give a HARD-NEWS story a SOFT-NEWS ANGLE

filter a plastic or glass device attached to the lens of a camera to correct or enhance lighting

fighting words expressions that might disrupt school routine—usually insults based on race, ethnicity, religion, or sex

film a thin piece of plastic coated with silver particles that darken when exposed to light. Film is used in a standard (nondigital) camera to create images of a scene photographed by the camera.

film processing developing and printing photographs from FILM

film speed a FILM rating, indicated by a number, that reflects a film's sensitivity to light. The lower the number, the "slower" the film and the less sensitive it is to light.

filter question a type of SURVEY question used to weed out answers that won't be meaningful

5 W's and H the journalist's main questions: *who, what, when, where, why,* and *how*

flare in photography, an effect that occurs when a photographer shoots into the sun, creating a series of bright white circles in the image. A LENS HOOD can help prevent flare.

flush-left alignment vertical ALIGNMENT along a left margin

flush-right alignment vertical ALIGNMENT along a right margin

focal length in a camera, the measurement of the LENS in millimeters. The lower the lens number, the shorter the focal length. The shorter the focal length, the wider the lens.

fold the middle of a page where large-format newspapers are folded

folio a page number. The folio often includes the name and section of the paper as well.

follow-up question an INTERVIEW question intended to get a SOURCE to further explain or expand upon a previous answer

follow-up story a story that follows up on a previously reported story

font a complete set of CHARACTERS in one size and style of a TYPEFACE, such as 12-point Gill Sans Italic. Type size is measured in POINTS. Type style refers to the WEIGHT, WIDTH, and POSTURE of a character.

force-justified alignment ALIGNMENT along the right and left margins despite gaps in the type that create WHITE SPACE

format the physical size of a newspaper page

front lighting in photography, lighting in which the light source is behind the photographer so the subject is evenly lit from the front

f-stop in a camera, a setting that indicates the APERTURE (LENS opening) in numbers. The lower the number, the wider the aperture.

future book a listing of events, by date, that may be covered in future issues of a newspaper

graphic or **art** a photograph, illustration, or device such as a line, box, screen, chart, graph, diagram, map, or arrow

greeting in a sales presentation, the friendly hello, followed by an identification of the salesperson, the newspaper, and the purpose of the visit

grid a pattern of lines that forms the base for placing visual elements on a newspaper page. Vertical lines show the COLUMN width and space between columns. Horizontal lines are typically at one-inch increments.

grid sheet a sheet, the size of a specific newspaper FORMAT, lined with light-colored GRID marks. Grid sheets are used as a form on which to make DUMMIES.

gutter WHITE SPACE that separates COLUMNS and FACING PAGES

halftone a photograph made from a photograph, shot through a special screen that converts the original image into a series of dots. The printed dots blend together into the photographic image when they're viewed from a normal distance.

hammerhead a type of HEADLINE that consists of a word or brief phrase set in large, bold type above a longer, lighter main headline

hard copy a paper copy

hard news factual reporting of current important news; also called *straight news*

headline a very brief description of a story printed in larger type, usually above the story

historical feature a FEATURE story about an interesting aspect of a historical topic, gathered from research and interviews

how-to feature a FEATURE story that explains how to do something

human interest an ELEMENT OF NEWS that refers to the part of a story that deals with human lives and emotions

human-interest feature a short FEATURE story, told in a unique and clever way, that concentrates on an unusual and emotionally appealing subject (person, place, object, or animal)

icon a graphic symbol

identification in a DISPLAY AD, the COPY that tells the advertiser's name, address, phone, and other contact details

in-depth reporting a style of reporting that goes deep beneath the surface of a topic. In-depth stories require extensive research, many interviews, and dozens of SOURCES.

index COPY that lists the page numbers on which each section starts

indirect quote a paraphrase, or summary, of the meaning of a DIRECT QUOTE, reworded by the reporter

infographic a GRAPHIC that presents statistical information, such as a map, chart, diagram, or time line

informative feature a FEATURE story that presents practical information on an interesting topic

initial cap or **drop cap** a large capital letter of the opening word in a story, which serves as a GRAPHIC and an ENTRY POINT

internal margin a consistent margin of WHITE SPACE between COPY and GRAPHICS. It's usually one PICA in width.

internship a usually unpaid position at a professional newspaper or other business, taken for the purpose of gaining valuable experience

interview a situation in which a reporter asks a SOURCE questions and records the answers, which may be used later in a NEWS story

invasion of privacy unlawful prying by the government and the media into the lives of private citizens

inverted pyramid a style of reporting in which the most important information comes first. In each successive paragraph the information is a little less important.

investigative reporting a type of IN-DEPTH REPORTING that seeks to uncover and expose something hidden. In many cases, what is revealed is illegal activity or information that has been purposely kept from the public.

issue number a number that refers to the consecutive number of issues of a publication during one calendar year

jargon technical or specialized language

jump to continue a story onto another page

jumphead a line of COPY that shows a reader where to start reading a JUMPED story again

jumpline a line of COPY that indicates the page on which a story continues

justified alignment ALIGNMENT along the left and right margins

kicker a type of HEADLINE that consist of a word or brief phrase set above a longer, main headline

layout the design stage where all the elements of a newspaper's pages are arranged; the physical arrangement of the elements on a page

lead the beginning of a newspaper story that leads readers into the story

leading or **linespacing** the space between the BASELINE of one line of COPY and the baseline of the next, measured in POINTS

leg a vertical COLUMN of COPY, referred to by its length in inches (for example, "4-inch leg")

lens the part of a camera through which light enters, is sharpened, and is transmitted to the FILM or solar cell

lens hood a device that shields a lens from direct sun to prevent FLARE

letter to the editor a short letter from a reader expressing an opinion

letterspacing extra space between letters in a line of COPY

libel false published material that damages the reputation of a person, business, or product

literary magazine a magazine containing fiction, poetry, art, and photography

local angle someone or something that connects a story's topic to the local readers

localize to give a story a LOCAL ANGLE

logo an identification mark, usually consisting of COPY combined with a GRAPHIC

mainbar a main story, distinguished from a SIDEBAR

managing editor on some newspapers, the person who manages the day-to-day operations of a newspaper

masthead a boxed item that gives important information about the newspaper

misquote to change the words or meaning of a QUOTE, either intentionally or by accident

modem a device that converts COPY and GRAPHICS into signals that can be sent and received over phone lines

modular design a style of page LAYOUT that uses rectangular or square units. Each unit consists of all the visual elements that make up the layout for a particular story.

morgue a collection of back issues of the newspaper, needed for reference and historical record

mugshot or **headshot** a photo that shows only the shoulders and head of a person

nameplate or **flag** COPY (often combined with a GRAPHIC) that states the name of the newspaper in large bold letters across the front page. It includes the VOLUME NUMBER and ISSUE NUMBER, publication date, and city and state where the paper is published.

negative a frame of processed FILM that shows the reverse of light and dark areas that will appear in the printed photograph

news information about events, people, or issues that the public wants or needs to know

news brief a short, condensed NEWS story

news feature a FEATURE story that offer a HUMAN-INTEREST view of a HARD-NEWS event

news magazine a newspaper FORMAT that measures 8 1/2 by 11 inches

news peg the connection of a FEATURE story to a related NEWS item

news release information about an organization provided to the news media by that organization

newsworthy having most of the ELEMENTS OF NEWS, or being something most readers would want or need to know

novelty a class of type that reflects a particular mood or historic period

nut graph the paragraph that contains the core—or most important information—of a story

obscenity material considered offensive by community standards and lacking any serious literary, artistic, political, or scientific value

off the record an agreement between a SOURCE and a reporter that specifies restrictions on how the reporter may use information from the source

op-ed page short for opposite-editorial page

open-ended question an INTERVIEW question that allows the SOURCE to form a detailed response. Open-ended questions can't be answered by one word, such as *yes* or *no*.

opposite lead a LEAD that cites one point of view and follows it with the opposite point of view

orphan a small word at the end of a paragraph, sitting on a line by itself; also called a WIDOW.

overprint the printing of one item on top of another

page proof a version of edited COPY that has been placed in a designed page. A page proof shows how the page will look when it's printed or photocopied.

pan in photography, to follow a subject by moving a camera at the same pace and direction as the subject. This creates a photograph in which the subject is in focus but the background is blurred.

partial quote the key words or the most revealing phrases from a DIRECT QUOTE, which are then included as part of an INDIRECT QUOTE.

paste-up the process of building the actual newspaper pages from the DUMMIES; the finished pages, ready for the printer

personal-accomplishment feature a FEATURE story that focuses on an individual who accomplished something amazing or overcame a particular life struggle

personal ad little notes from one person to another that are sometimes published in a classified ad section

personality profile a FEATURE story that reveals the personality of a someone through incidents, ANECDOTES, and QUOTES

photo credit a line of COPY that identifies the photographer of a particular photo

photo essay an arrangement of photos (typically three to seven) centered around an event or a theme. A photo essay may tell a developing story.

photo release a form that gives a photographer permission to take and use a photo of someone taken in a nonpublic place

photojournalism telling the NEWS through photographs

pica a designer's measurement equaling one-sixth of an inch. There are 6 picas in an inch and 12 POINTS in a pica.

pica stick a ruler used in graphic arts that shows PICAS and inches

pitch in a DISPLAY AD, the COPY that tells readers information about a product or service

point a designer's measurement. There are 72 points in an inch and 12 points in a PICA.

point-counterpoint articles two or more BYLINED opinion articles, written by people on opposite sides of an issue, and printed side by side

postgame story a COVERAGE STORY about a sports event. Postgame stories are nearly always FEATURIZED and should emphasize the drama of the event with an ANGLE that recaptures the atmosphere of the event and the emotion of critical moments.

posture the slant of a letter. A right slant is referred to by the term *italic* or *oblique*. An upright posture is referred to as *roman*.

pregame story an ADVANCE STORY about a sports event. Pregame stories include the 5 W'S AND H early in the story. They're generally FEATURIZED and have a unique ANGLE.

press the machine that prints the newspaper

press run the number of copies of a newspaper printed for a single issue

primary source a resource that offers the best and most reliable source of essential information on a topic. A primary source is often a person or document that provides firsthand information or expert knowledge on a topic.

prior review a situation in which a principal or other authority reviews a publication before it's printed

privilege the defense to libel in which all information presented in legal or official proceedings and reports is immune from libel as long as the account is fair and accurate

production the entire process of preparing the pages for the printer or the photocopier

prominence an ELEMENT OF NEWS that indicates how well known someone or something is to the readers

proof a version of edited COPY

proofread the process of reading PROOFS to correct mechanical errors made by a writer or COPY EDITOR

proximity an ELEMENT OF NEWS that indicates the geographic nearness of someone or something to the readers

public figure a person who purposely thrusts himself or herself into the NEWS

public forum a place to freely exchange ideas

public official a government official—for example, a mayor, a school board president, and so on

public-service announcement (PSA) an ad that delivers a message from a nonprofit organization

publisher the head of the entire newspaper operation. On school papers, the publisher is the school administration, represented by the adviser.

pull quote a QUOTE taken from a story and arranged as a GRAPHIC in the LAYOUT of the story

punch lead a LEAD that opens with an amazing fact or startling statement that arouses reader interest

Q & A format a story format that shows both the questions and the answers of an interview.

question lead a LEAD that begins with a question to the reader. This type of lead should be used only if the question is compelling and is the focus of the story.

questionnaire a written SURVEY

quick-read menu a type of SIDEBAR that offers a brief selection of specialized information

quote the exact wording of a statement from a SOURCE

quote lead a LEAD that begins with a QUOTE from someone featured in the story. This type of lead should be used only if the quote is a unique, fascinating statement that can stand on its own.

random sample a significant segment of a group chosen at random for a SURVEY. Each person in a random sample must have an equal chance of being surveyed.

random-opinion poll a popular type of opinion article. It poses a question on an EDITORIAL topic to a small group of people representing a range of opinions. Each person's opinion is printed, often next to his or her photo.

rate sheet information about ad rates, distributed to advertising clients

refer a line of COPY that points readers to a related story elsewhere in the issue

reflector in photography, a device that reflects light from the light source back onto the subject to fill in details hidden by shadow

registration the correct positioning of elements in a printed image

repetition the design principle that reflects the recurring use of visual arrangements to create order in a design

retraction a published correction of an error made in a publication

reverse print light type on a dark background

review a BYLINED opinion article focusing on the relative worth of a product or performance

right of reply permitting a person or organization criticized in a story the chance to respond to that criticism in the same story

roving reporter in school papers, a series of very short (one- and two-sentence) NEWS reports. Each report is separated by an ellipsis (. . .).

rule a thin vertical or horizontal line that serves to accent or separate elements. Its width is measured in POINTS.

rule of thirds a method of arranging the visual elements of a photograph. The photographer places the main subject on one of the intersecting points of a grid formed by dividing the frame into thirds horizontally and vertically.

run sheet a listing of ad sales and their placement within the newspaper

running features a FEATURE of a particular type that appears, or runs, in each issue

saddle-stitch binding a method of binding pages together with staples down the center of all FACING PAGES

sales kit in ad sales, a packet of information used in a sales presentation

sales pitch in a sales presentation, an explanation of the benefits of buying a product or service

sans serif a class of type without serifs

scanner a device similar to a photocopying machine, except that it converts a physical object or image into an electronic image

scenic lead a LEAD that uses a description of the scene or environment in which an event took place

screen a shaded area. The darkness or lightness of the screen is measured in percentages.

script a class of type that resembles handwriting

secondary source a resource that offers reliable secondhand information on a topic

section editor or **page editor** an editor who oversees the reporting and production of a particular section of the newspaper

sensationalism the tendency to publish information that creates intense but brief interest or emotional reaction

serif a class of type with small “feet” or strokes at the end of most letters

shared-experience feature a FEATURE story that shares information gained from the writer’s firsthand experience in doing something

shoot a formally arranged photo session

shutter in a camera, a device that slides back and forth to control the amount of time the FILM or solar cell is exposed to light

shutter release in a camera, a mechanism to release the SHUTTER

shutter speed in a camera, a setting that indicates how fast the SHUTTER opens and closes, measured in fractions of a second. The higher (or faster) the shutter speed, the less light is let in through the shutter.

sidebar a story that's closely related to, or adds to, the main story, or MAINBAR

side lighting in photography, lighting in which the light source is to one side of the camera

signature a printed page that has been folded for binding

size to enlarge or reduce a photograph to fit into a certain space on the page

slander false spoken statements that damage the reputation or a person, business, or product

slick a CAMERA-READY GRAPHIC to be placed in an ad

slogan in a DISPLAY AD, a short catchy phrase that identifies a product with its advertiser

slug a word or phrase that identifies a story or other COPY

soft news reporting that entertains and informs. It usually appeals to the emotions and is less current and important than HARD NEWS.

source a resource that provides reliable, truthful information about a topic

specs or **specifications** information about what an ad or other page element should say and how it should look on the page

spot color one color applied in strategic places on a page

spread a set of FACING PAGES

standing head a HEADLINE for a regular feature in each issue of a newspaper

storytelling format a form of reporting in which the information is presented as a narrative story

storytelling lead a LEAD that uses a dramatic, narrative style to introduce the main characters, the conflict, and perhaps the setting of the story

stringer a freelance reporter (one who is not on staff) who contributes stories to a newspaper from time to time

style the way COPY should be written to be consistent within a publication. Rules for a publication's style are included in a STYLEBOOK.

stylebook a document that specifies a newspaper's rules for grammar, punctuation, and usage

subhead a miniheadline that indicates what the next section of COPY contains

subscription an arrangement in which a reader pays in advance to receive a publication on a regular basis for a certain period of time

summary lead a factual, to-the-point LEAD that provides a basic summary of the story in as few words as possible

survey or **poll** a report of what people in a specific group feel or think about a topic

tabloid a newspaper FORMAT that measures approximately 11 by 17 inches

tearsheet the page torn from a newspaper, on which a particular client's ad appears

teaser copy that promotes stories inside the issue

telegram method a method for writing HEADLINES in which a writer trims the headline to essential words that indicate the main point of the story

telephoto lens a LENS that has a long FOCAL LENGTH. It magnifies the elements of a scene, making them appear crowded together and closer to the camera than they actually are.

thumbnail a small, rough sketch representing a page LAYOUT

timeliness an ELEMENT OF NEWS that indicates how current or new something is

tip a piece of information that leads a reporter to a potential story

tombstoning the placing of two HEADLINES side by side

transitions the links between ideas within paragraphs and from one paragraph to the next

trapped white space an empty block of space boxed into the middle of a page

tripod a two-part HEADLINE that consists of a word or brief phrase set in large, bold type alongside a two-line headline that's equal in height to the first part; a three-legged device on which a camera can be mounted for the purpose of shooting at slow SHUTTER SPEEDS without moving the camera

typeface a design of a complete set of type CHARACTERS, specified by a name, such as Arial or Garamond

typography the way printed letters are handled on a page

unity the design principle that reflects a striving for a sense of wholeness—so each part of a design looks different, yet all have the same visual tone, or feeling

upstyle a style of HEADLINE in which every major word is capitalized

viewfinder in a camera, a framing device that allows the photographer to see the picture before it's taken

volume number a number that refers to the number of years a newspaper has been in existence

webmaster a person who writes, edits, designs, and maintains a web site

weight the visual width of the strokes that make up each letter. *Light, medium, demibold, bold,* and *extrabold* are terms used to describe the weight of a TYPEFACE.

white space empty (blank) area on a page

wide-angle lens a LENS that has a short FOCAL LENGTH. This type of lens takes in more of a scene than a narrower lens does. But it stretches perspective, making the visual elements in a scene appear farther apart than they are in reality.

widow a short line at the end of a paragraph appearing at the top of a page or COLUMN

width the horizontal measure of a type CHARACTER. *Condensed* and *extended* are terms used to describe the width of a TYPEFACE.

wrap-up in a sales presentation, a review of the transaction and plans for the next contact or action

zine a magazine published on the Internet

zoom lens a variable-length LENS. It allows a photographer to vary the FOCAL LENGTH between WIDE-ANGLE and TELEPHOTO lengths.

Index

A

B

C

G

H

O

P

Q

T

U

V

W

Y

Z